D0442757

The Devil
Never Sleeps

and Other Essays

BOOKS BY ANDREI CODRESCU

MEMOIRS

Ay, Cuba! A Socio-Erotic Journey
Road Scholar
The Hole in the Flag: An Exile's Story of Return and Revolution
In America's Shoes
The Life and Times of an Involuntary Genius

ESSAYS

Hail Babylon!
The Dog with the Chip in his Neck
Zombification
The Muse is Always Half-Dressed in New Orleans
The Disappearance of the Outside
Raised by Puppets Only to be Killed by Research
A Craving for Swan

POETRY

Alien Candor
Belligerence
Comrade Past and Mister Present
Selected Poems: 1970–1980
Diapers on the Snow
Necrocorrida
For the Love of a Coat
The Lady Painter
The Marriage of Insult and Injury
A Mote Suite for Jan and Anselm
Grammar and Money
A Serious Morning
Secret Training
the, here, what, where
The History of the Growth of Heaven
License to Carry a Gun

FICTION

A Bar in Brooklyn
Messiah
The Blood Countess
Monsieur Teste in America and Other Instances of Realism
The Repentance of Lorraine
Why I Can't Talk on the Telephone

The Devil
Never Sleeps

and Other Essays

Andrei Codrescu

St. Martin's Press ❧ New York

Design by Maureen Troy

Library of Congress Cataloging-in-Publication Data
Codrescu, Andrei.
   The Devil never sleeps : and other essays / Andrei Codrescu.—1st ed.
      p.   cm.
   ISBN 0-312-20294-6
      I. Title.

   PS3553.O3 D4 2000
   814'.54—dc21

                                                            99-055765

First Edition: March 2000

10 9 8 7 6 5 4 3 2 1

Contents

Part Three: *The Devil in Eastern Europe, One of his Ancestral Homes*

Part Four: *The Devil's Art: Autobiography*

Part Five: *Amnesia of the Body Politic*

Part Six: *Virtuality Takes Command*

Part One

I Have Been Warned

to Stay Away

from Eschatology:

I Can't Do It[*]

---

[*]In December 1995 National Public Radio broadcast my commentary gently deriding the Christian fundamentalist belief known as the Rapture, an event prior to the Apocalypse, during which all true believers would be suctioned off to heaven in a single whoosh, leaving behind their cars, their work desks, and their interlocutors.

The Rapture was so imminent that many believers sported bumper stickers that said IN CASE OF RAPTURE THIS CAR WILL BE UNMANNED. I pointed out the Raptured's considerable amount of crude disregard for their fellow beings. My radio commentary engendered a vast protest organized by Ralph Reed of the Christian Coalition. Forty thousand letters of protest reached NPR and Congress, accusing me of anti-Christian bias. The protest took issue with the very existence of public broadcasting, as exemplified by demons like myself. In the end, NPR apologized for my remarks, and every one of those forty thousand letters was answered. In the wake of this unusual outpouring of sentiment, I was warned anonymously by either well-meaning or ill-wishing parties to "stay away from eschatology." Alas.

The Devil Never Sleeps

The Devil never sleeps because he's got too much to do and the things he's already done keep him awake. So the Devil is no different from your average American with too much to do and too much to think about. If there is a difference between the Devil and the average Joe, it is only that the Devil feels no guilt. On the contrary, what keeps him awake at night is the pleasure of remembering, living his deeds all over again. The Devil uses insomnia to live twice, while the average Joe just breaks into a cold sweat.

People once believed seriously in the Devil, so when bad things happened they knew who was responsible for them. Many bad things happened back then, so many that a whole class of church people existed whose only job was to keep track of all the bad things and their degree of badness. Not all things were equally bad. Some bad things that happened to one personally, such as disease and death, were the work of God because they were part of the pattern of common life. Bigger bad things, such as famines, plague, or earthquakes, could have been God's or the Devil's, depending on how wicked or God-fearing people were. If people were God-fearing and bad things happened to them, then it was Devil's work. And twice vice versa. If the bad things that happened to the community were the Devil's work, then the Devil's agents who had caused these things (the Devil used human

3

"minions" to do his dirty work) had to be found and burned alive. Burning alive the Devil's agents was God's work and it made people happy. The Devil rather enjoyed seeing his minions burn, so nobody was the worse for it, except the people burning. It was a win-win situation for the living.

The Devil started losing friends and influence in the eighteenth century, when people discovered that many bad things had no single author. French philosophers, in particular, took some spirited whacks at both God and the Devil, though most of them—Voltaire, for instance—found the Devil a much more personable figure than his counterpart. The Devil shed much of his dreadfulness for the upper classes, mutating into a sympathetic, carnival-esque character, whose job was to suggest titillating possibilities. Sex and food, or lust and gluttony, lost their sinful terror and became delightful pur-suits. Casanova's memoir, *The Story of My Life,* chronicles, with methodical thoroughness and utter lack of regret, his lifelong indulgences. Casanova wrote his memoir in old age, thus reliving his devilish life during long in-somniac nights. The Devil's best champion was the Marquis de Sade, who methodically reversed the teachings of the Church to produce pornographic parables curiously devoid of prurience. In De Sade's methodical work of virtue-demolition, the Devil is revealed as a logician and a grammarian. De Sade's works, written mostly in prison, capture the antagonists in balance.

After the eighteenth century, the Devil got more and more ragged around the edges, like a plush toy kicked around too long by rough children. By the end of the nineteenth century he barely had a place to live: most of the world had been discovered, even the scariest forests, and men's souls were being taken apart by psychology. From carnival to operetta to a banal figure of speech, the Devil seemed to be nearly extinct. And then, surprise! Hitler! The sleeping bourgeoisie, safely ensconced in its ideas of reason and progress, gave birth to the Devil. Hitler embodied every repressed aspect of the Devil since the early Middle Ages. All that had been laughed away came back concentrated inside a little man with a tiny mustache who mag-netized all the unfocused evil in the world and made the business of hell both serious and modern. Hitler was the classic Devil of the early Church, ignorant, bloody, banal, bureaucratic. He was part gargoyle, part Luther.

In the Christian world, until the Reformation, the Devil was as serious as the political climate. The Church portrayed him as adaptable. He was in-sidious and ready to take on as much credibility as was required by the Pope. This combination of adaptability and insatiability pointed to two crucial models for the Devil: women and Jews. In his development, the Devil took on women because they were accessible through lust ("weaker vessels") and Jews, because they could spread far and wide the Devil's dispatches. In the Middle Ages, the Devil looked physically like a Jew, a pictorial and psychological resemblance that was invented by Lutherans and carried forward all the way into Hitler's gas ovens. This fate might have befallen women as well if they hadn't been needed to propagate the race. As it was, only a number of women ("witches" and "temptresses") were chosen to pay for their connection with the Devil, standing in symbolically for all womankind. The Christian Devil never ceased acting in the subconscious of Western people, even though he was greatly neutralized after the end of the seventeenth century. In the eighteenth century, when people were actually reasonable for a few minutes, he began receding again.

When the Inquisition, which was the preeminent detector of witches and falsely converted Jews, lost its efficacy in Europe, it attempted to set roots in the New World. It failed resolutely. The Spanish Crown sent an inquisitor to New Orleans, but the locals shipped him back on the same conveyance he arrived in. He returned years later, not an inquisitor any longer, and distinguished himself by good works among Native Americans. Still, the Devil did get a berth on the Mayflower and came here with the Puritans. After the bloodletting at Salem, the Puritan ethos went underground, whence it emerges at regular intervals in American political and cultural life. Two recent examples: Kenneth Starr's sexual witch hunt, and the prohibition against smoking in public places. The Devil is distinguished by his seductiveness and by the smoke that issues perpetually from his nostrils. Crusaders for so-called morality always take a stand against the Devil, though they often end up working in his interests.

In the closing days of the second Christian millennium, many people in the great democracy of America have started believing in the Devil again. Born-again Christians in this technologically advanced country have begun an unholy obsession with old Satan while, ironically, in less advanced parts of the world, superstitious Islamic fundamentalists believe that America is herself the Devil. No question about it, the Devil is back. He hatches and blooms in the bafflement wrought in the faithful by excessive technology.

For all that, the American Devil, a latecomer to these shores, evinces neither the highs nor the lows of the Satanic majesty honed over time in the cauldrons and on the gibbets of Europe. In this country, he neither raged insanely nor decayed properly, which is why he is still taken seriously. The aspect of the Enlightenment that struggled to diminish him had already won in Europe, leaving America free to take only the Enlightenment's most high-minded and reasonable principles to heart.

The Rolling Stones met with disaster in the U.S. in 1969, at Altamont, when they performed "Sympathy for the Devil." This had never happened in England. Marianne Faithfull, Mick Jagger's girlfriend at the time, explained that for the English the devil is a literary and comic figure, but that Americans take the devil seriously, which explains why the concert at Altamont appeared to many people to be the end of the peace-loving sixties, letting loose a decade of evil.[*]

I am both European and American, so the Devil is for me both comic and serious. While the Devil remains, for Christian fundamentalists, a unique generator of evil, he has by no means stayed still. He has evolved, technologically if not psychologically, to keep up with the times. The same cannot be said, alas, about God, who is behind the times. God's repertoire has been limited basically to the Ten Commandments and to permission (I hope!) for the use of his Son by televangelicals in pitches for money, and by politicals in pitches for power. God's granting of licenses on his Son is seemingly limitless, which somewhat dilutes the message.

The Devil has moved way ahead in both direct appearances and the streamlining of his vast operation. The Internet has been the Devil's greatest invention since television. There was a time, in the heyday of the Church in the fourteenth century, when God and the Devil were poised in a balance of powers resembling the MAD (Mutual Assured Destruction) policy of the Cold War. In those days, just like God, whose universe he mirrored, the Devil had scores of angels to produce the multitude of evils in the world. Like any bureaucracy, the Devil's production office had branches in charge of major activities, and these offices were efficient or inefficient depending on the angels who ran them. Evil angels, just like the good angels, had personalities: They were modest or profligate, expansive or uptight, cold or hot, sweet or sour, bitter or tart, sported a full suit of feathers, were nearly bald, etc, etc. In other words, they were as close to humans as they

---

[*]Marianne Faithfull and David Dalton, *Faithfull: An Autobiography* (New York: Little, Brown and Company, 1994).

could be. Everything was closer in those days: the sky, the stars, God, heaven, and hell. All you had to do back then was to stretch out your hand to brush it against something winged, furry, and uncanny.

Things are not so cozy for God anymore, but we are really tight with the Devil. Thanks to the movies, television, and the Internet, we can now view devils who look more familiar to us than the strange people sharing our couch. Thanks to the film director John Waters, we now know that the Devil can be a "serial mom," which is to say an ordinary, family-loving human being who lets out a bit of murderous steam when her chores are done. John Waters has illustrated remarkably the quality of evil in our time. As Hannah Arendt said, speaking of Nazis, evil is banal. "The banality of evil" is why many of us have no idea that it exists. The machinelike efficiency of Nazi Germany was just a modern bureaucracy.

There is a difference between the grim Devil of fundamentalist Christians and the ubiquitous Devil of our secular culture, as seen on television and movies. Of course, fundamentalists aren't fooled for a second: they can see his glowing paws in the dark, whether he wears gloves or silk stockings. The modern Devil operates both nakedly and in disguise. Nakedly, he speaks through secular humanists, one-world orderers (agents of ZOG—Zionist Occupation Government), Democrats, urban dwellers, clubbers of Rome, freemasons, Catholics, the Queen of England, rock 'n' roll, lab-coated scientists (both above and under the earth's crust), number crunchers, education boards, fetus killers, sexual deviants, media mavens, idolaters, image makers, evolutionists, and ironists. In disguise, he tries not to look or sound like any of the above to the extent that he sometimes sounds like a man of God. The Devil, as seen on television, at the movies, and on the Internet, is a multi-tentacled organism continually propagating its evil essences unto an innocent and corruptible body politic. Good Christians are not fooled by the multitude of the secular Devil's guises, whether he pops up in the news or masquerades as entertainment. But the poor secular Devil barely know that he's the Devil. He's just . . . secular. He depends on the Christian Coalition and its kin to recognize and identify him. His self-image depends on it.

A good student of the Devil knows that his job is to perpetuate this wicked world, which is why fornication is his favorite vice, and libido his medium. God, on the other hand, works to destroy the world in order to cleanse and purify it. This battle will be decided at Armageddon, at the coming of the millennium. On the subject of the millennium, there is disagreement, both about the date and about the sequence, but there is no mistaking the principal actors. The paranoids and the optimists, both secular and religious, are united in the belief of their righteousness. What follows is a classification of the righteous.

GENERAL DESCRIPTION:

The PARANOIDS are of three kinds: religious, secular, and technological. The religious paranoids are of three kinds, too: fundamentalist, New Ager, and paramilitary. The secular paranoids also have three branches: X-Filers, tabloidoids, and weekend satanists. The techno paranoids are divided also, like Gaul, into three parts: Y2K-ers, genetophobes, and ecodystopians.

The OPTIMISTS are likewise classifiable according to strict Linnaean principles and occasionally overlap the paranoids. The three kinds are: liberals, secularists, and utopians. Liberals are of three kinds: free-marketeers, one-worlders, and armchair philosophers. Secularists, who are sometimes liberals, have three branches: laissez-fairians, post-Enlightenmentarians, and statophile utopians. Utopians, who overlap the religious paranoids, divide as well into fundamentalists, New Agers, and post-history buffetarians.

Here is how their beliefs operate:

KINGDOM: PARANOIDS
GENUS: RELIGIOUS
SPECIES: FUNDAMENTALIST, NEW AGER, PARAMILITARY

Fundamentalists (God's party) are sure their scriptures are about to bear apocalyptic fruit and can't wait to see the rest of us burn in hell while they meet their Maker amid harp music and nard sprays.

New Agers (the Devil's party), informed by Nostradamus, astrology, oracles, private signs, misreadings of runes and glyphs, Kali Yuga, and various psychotics, can see the day of reckoning as surely as they can read their tea leaves.

Paramilitary (the God-Devil Party) paranoids are impatient fascists with a death wish who want to take the rest of us with them in a willed Armageddon.

KINGDOM: PARANOIDS
GENUS: SECULAR
SPECIES: X-FILERS, TABLOIDOIDS, WEEKEND SATANISTS

X-Filers are sure that the government is keeping secret the presence of aliens (devils) among us, and that the alliance of government (which may have already been taken over by aliens!) and an interplanetary invasion force, means that the human race is at an end.

Tabloidoids are broader-based X-Filers who add the Kennedy assassinations, the CIA, and any number of earth- or space-based conspiracies to bear on their feelings of total paranoid helplessness.

Weekend Satanists are working-class and lower-middle-class pale white people who can be Goths, vampires, space creatures, or a sci-fi combination of all of them, who have invested their minds and bodies into an aesthetic that impatiently awaits the Next Life.

KINGDOM: PARANOIDS
GENUS: TECHNOLOGICAL
SPECIES: Y2K-ERS, GENETOPHOBES, ECODYSTOPIANS

Y2K-ers are the descendants of the 1950s A-bomb shelterians (who are themselves the descendants of hoarding Puritans). They are stockpiling Campbell's soups, weapons, and very bad novels, in expectation of a prolonged apocalypse brought about by the failure of their computers to download porn and process their bank statements.

Genetophobes are spawns of Molly the Cloned Sheep and readers of newspapers who see genetic engineering making the one or two fatal leaps into obliterating humanity.

Ecodystopians see the planet reaching its expiration date thanks to environmental alteration, pollution, overpopulation, and engineered viruses.

KINGDOM: OPTIMISTS
GENUS: LIBERALS
SPECIES: FREE-MARKETEERS

Free-market liberals believe in the Invisible Hand of Adam Smith but have a gnawing suspicion that the Hand might be giving the finger to a lot of people, so they pay lip service to environmental causes (leaving the children "a livable planet") while wallowing quite indiscriminately in the ever-rising Market (the Devil).

KINGDOM: OPTIMISTS
GENUS: LIBERALS
SPECIES: ONE-WORLDERS

One-worlders believe in the Global Economy and Technology, the new Esperanto. They argue that trade barriers must come down before physical borders do. Their future world has the United States (the new Jerusalem or Rome) shining on the hill, while all good things flow from it to the provinces.

KINGDOM: OPTIMISTS
GENUS: LIBERALS
SPECIES: ARMCHAIR PHILOSOPHERS

Armchair philosophers are an ever-increasing tribe of liberal utopians who absorb and regurgitate every optimistic signal coming from the above groups, and spread them through their circles with support from PBS and the Internet. Their portfolios aren't shabby, but they aren't big enough to cause them to be active. The APs are the descendants of Chekhov's turn-of-the-nineteenth-century Russian provincials. They live in small towns (where the Devil does the most damage).

KINGDOM: OPTIMISTS
GENUS: SECULARISTS
SPECIES: LAISSEZ-FAIRIANS

Laissez-fairians are active proponents of doing nothing and forgetting everything, especially religious quarrels. In real life, they tend to be casual Unitarians (Devil worshippers).

KINGDOM: OPTIMISTS
GENUS: SECULARISTS
SPECIES: POST-ENLIGHTENMENTARIANS

Post-Enlightenmentarians are hedonists. They enjoy surfing, group marriage, anti-aging vitamins, cryogenics, and Internet porn. They originated in California, but they can be found as far north as Maine. Their goal is physical immortality. (The Devil loves them the best.)

KINGDOM: OPTIMISTS
GENUS: SECULARISTS
SPECIES: STATOPHILE UTOPIANS

Statophile Utopians cite statistics proving that things are getting better, even if for them, personally, things might be getting worse. SUs are quaint and their numbers dwindle and increase, depending on the newspaper they read (Bourgeois devilitarians).

KINGDOM: OPTIMISTS
GENUS: UTOPIANS
SPECIES: FUNDAMENTALISTS

Like their paranoid kin, the optimistic fundamentalists see the end of the world as an opportunity for the coming of the Kingdom. Unlike their kin, they dwell less on the Horrors of the End and more on the Benefits of the New. Some of them even believe that Christ has already come and that we already live in Paradise, only we don't know it (Insufficiently attuned to the Devil).

KINGDOM: OPTIMISTS
GENUS: UTOPIANS
SPECIES: NEW AGERS

Like their paranoid kin, the optimistic New Agers point to signs, portents, coffee grounds, aliens, and genetics to prove that physical and spiritual immortality are established facts. One meets many such believers in New Age summer camps on the East and West coasts. (They are the Devil's children: his kindergartens are overflowing.)

KINGDOM: OPTIMISTS
GENUS: UTOPIANS
SPECIES: POST-HISTORY BUFFETARIANS

Buffetarians partake of a buffet of all the above, in the manner of a smorgasbord or a cruise through ethnic cuisines. Their temperaments are essentially sunny, so they'll pick anything that makes them feel better, without particular bias for any of them. (The Devil is in the spices.)

Let us now have a look at the original description of the End of the Christian World, involving the Final Battle between God and the Devil, which is the spring of both our paranoia and optimism (after the paranoia has subsided).

The Revelation of St. John

The visions of John of Patmos have been scaring Christians for nearly two millennia. Two thousand years ago, John, a Greek recluse on the island of Patmos, wrote the last book of the Bible. John called his vision "Revelation," because angels parted the curtains of time for him, revealing the cosmic drama in exact and pitiless detail. John was not simply a prophet, he was an interactive spectator to events that he then described in the past tense, though they were yet to occur. John witnessed the destruction of the world and the end of time from a front-row seat. He was prey to the terror, nausea, and exaltation of the witness. The imperative to describe what he saw conflicted with his all-too-human desire to flee the theater and purge himself of the eschatological vision. After witnessing the end of humanity, the destruction of the earth, and the abolishment of time, John was given a little book by an angel who told him, "Eat it up and it shall make thy belly bitter, but it shall be in thy mouth sweet as honey." At this point, John barely had the stomach to go on looking, even though the promised message would be as sweet as honey. He had to keep witnessing and describing until the Redemption.

The "little book" was given to John at a midway point in the cosmic drama—worse was yet to come. It was a long way to Redemption: the destruction of time was to be followed by the destruction of memory, the complete erasure of human history. But even that was not yet the End, because God's own tools of destruction, his prophets and saints, had to be destroyed because they had been contaminated by the evil they had helped vanquish. The Revelation abounds in false endings because God's wrath is insatiable and the True End will not come until God has reversed every trick of his creation and rooted it down to the seed. It is during these reversals that John makes his appearances, advising us of his fear and trembling. Nonetheless, he goes on to witness things inconceivably more dreadful, but ever more precise, more structurally harmonious, more daring. The cosmic punishments and battles that were, in the beginning, rooted in the psychology of men's weaknesses become slowly transmuted into an elemental order that flirts with chaos and transcends it.

The Revelation begins where most human imaginations fail, though human elements are still recognizable. John is vouchsafed the awesome vision of God, the "alpha and the omega," the creator and the destroyer, the beginning and the end. In the course of what is to come, God takes on many aspects: the Spirit, Christ, the Lamb, even the Beast. As Christ, the Spirit begins, reasonably enough, with complaints to and about those entrusted to carry his message, namely the Ten Churches. His churches have been contaminated by fornication, sacrifices to Balaam, failure to wash, falsity, pretense, greed, lack of passion, and lack of will. He offers them a pretty good deal: repent, and you will go to Paradise and get to eat fruit from the Tree of Life. More immediately, there will be other rewards for repentance: manna to eat, a cleansing white stone with a "new name" written on it, the "morning star," food, and jewels.

John is here, as elsewhere, very specific: he lists every particular. John is especially punctilious about numbers and measurements. His slide rule and his abacus are always at hand, even in the midst of the most desolate carnage. Seven is his favorite number. There are seven lamps, seven spirits, seven seals, seven horns, seven eyes, seven angels, seven trumpets, seven heads, seven crowns. He's also fond of four, ten, and twenty-four. Four beasts, four angels, four horses, four horsemen, four winds, ten churches, ten horns, twenty-four elders. John's favorite fraction is one-third. The destruction of the world proceeds by thirds: the First Angel burns up one-third of the earth; the Second Angel burns up one-third of the sea, kills one-third of the life in the sea, and destroys one-third of all ships; the Third Angel kills one-third of people by causing the Wormwood Star to make the waters bitter; the Fourth Angel kills one-third of the sun so there is no more light on earth. This divine numerology sets up the architecture for the brilliant hall of horrors and mirrors that is to follow.

The "carrot-and-stick" policy offered to churches out of the way, the second curtain opens and the Spirit gets down. We are now treated to the awesome complexity of the heavens, with its myriad of angels, thrones, beasts, churches, and spirits. Each member of the divine edifice has specific jobs in the coming devastation, which unfolds, curtain after curtain, or layer after layer, until the blinding core of the Heavenly Jerusalem is exposed at the heart of the universe. What occurs at each stage has been subject to myriad interpretations, but the scenes have never lost their luster. There is never one Death, there must always be a second Death. There is never one battle, there are always others. Even at the very End, when Satan has been vanquished and relegated in chains to the Bottomless Pit, there is the suggestion of another End. Satan will be imprisoned only for one thousand years. After that, he will come again, and the whole terrifying cycle of destruction and redemption will begin anew.

It is easy to see why readers of the Revelation have found there all the proof they needed for every paranoid fantasy. If the numbers alone don't do the job, the numberless beasts and angels fold neatly into the intuitive geometry built into us all. The Revelation is a mirror of the crystal connecting our oldest brain, the one that had witnessed great cataclysms, with the neocortex that promised deliverance from nature. Oddly enough, the line between the divine and the human is drawn physically by tattoos. Only those marked by God on the forehead with his own bar code may see the coming of Salvation. Others, who have tattooed their bodies with the aesthetic of the Beast, will be doomed. Tattoos, like numbers, pillars, and the entire hierarchy of heaven and hell, are the reiteration of a consistent and classical aesthetic. John's Revelation stands between the classicism of the Parthenon and the emotional exaltation of Gothic. The drama of the Revelation is Greek, but the sensibility is psychedelic.

The passage of time has not diminished the power of John's Revelation. It haunts our fin-de-millennium as strongly as it haunted the last fin-de-millennium, when humanity had neither penicillin nor computers. If anything, we can see more clearly now the perfect architecture of the prophecy, the crystalline structure of the events, their suspenseful unfolding and relentless rhythm. It is precisely because of our new insight into the structures of the brain, life, and the cosmos that we can better appreciate their terrifying poetry.

By the time John wrote the Revelation, the Beast was well developed. To find its roots one has to go much further back, when it barely had a name.

> Now therefore write ye this song for you, and teach it to the children of Israel: put it in their mouths, that this song may be a witness for me against the children of Israel.

> —Deuteronomy 31.19

This is one of the Torah's heaviest passages, in every sense: weight, gravity, and import. The weight of it is enormous: God tells Moses that it's time to retire and prepare his successor, Joshua; that God will personally see to it that the people cross over Jordan into the Promised Land; that he will aid them in destroying the people already there; that the people will grow forgetful; that he will hide his face from them in anger; and he gives Moses a poem (or song) to be read (or sung) publicly every seven years to remind people that he is the only God.

Literally, that's heavy. Moses has the burden of resigning, of insuring a successful succession, of reassuring the people, and of insuring that God's poem is placed in the Ark of the Covenant with the right instructions. Joshua's burden is to take the reins of power from the nearest-to-God and to persuade the people that the crossing and the coming battles will be won. The people's burden is to trust blindly in Moses' word, to accept Joshua, to have faith, to play out the destiny laid out by God, and to listen to the poem every seven years. God's burden is to put up with this unfaithful people and to hold on to the strictest interpretation of the covenant, with all the tiresome clauses of punishment and reward.

These are the burdens, the weight.

The gravity of the passage is retroactive, present, and forward into the future. When this was written, the events it describes had already happened. God's scenario had come to pass exactly the way he'd presented it to Moses. There are two ways of looking at this:

1) The truth of it is evident: the people under Joshua were successful. The Promised Land was a reality. The writer had no need of making the story fit the reality.

2) The times of the scribe were bad; the existence of the people and their divine right to the Promised Land were in jeopardy; God's command to Moses had to be told so as to renew the fighting spirit. But, essentially, it

does not matter. The Event itself is eternally present because it is the foundation of the legitimacy of the people. Retroactively, the Event recapitulates Moses' entire relationship with God from the very beginning and thus the people's relationship with God. The forward projection insures that every time Deuteronomy is read or God's poem recited, the Event becomes present.

The import of the passage is that it establishes once and for all the divine links between God and his people, between the people and their land, and between the people and their religious leaders.

The weightiness thus established, the questions begin.

1) Why do God and Moses keep meeting behind the bushes, at night, in secret? Why does God have to keep disguising himself? Since God's words to Moses seem clearly intended for all the people, why does he have to whisper them to Moses in the middle of the night? Why not just boom them out to everybody, thereby increasing his awesomeness and credibility?

In this instance, God first speaks to Moses alone and tells him that it's time to retire. Then God has him bring Joshua to the Tent of the Meeting at night where he shows himself in the shape of a cloud.

Two subquestions:

a) Did Moses make up God?

b) Did God and Moses have a carnal relationship?

Speculation:

a) Moses may have written the Laws, Moses may have composed the poem. Moses may have been a great writer. Who can vouch for his story? Again, we can look retroactively and say, "The story has come to pass; that is the proof of its divine origin." But perhaps the story had come to pass and then, only then, was the story written. Perhaps a writer as great as Moses looked back on the writer Moses and gave him divine certification. In the beginning, after all, was the Word. This story of receding writers does, in the end (and in the beginning), lead to a story-telling creator. Once again, it does not matter. Whoever wrote it made sure that the story would not be forgotten, through the use of such skillful mnemonic devices as a poem that pops up every seven years. This is the kind of story that, if repeated sufficiently, hardwires a tribe for business. If Moses made up God, he did it unconsciously. There is no doubt that Moses believed that he was hearing God speak to him and through him. And if a voice be this successful, it can only be God.

b) God displays every human attribute, especially jealousy, and later in history he has a Son. Is it not possible that something went down between him and humans that wasn't mere spirit intimacy? After all, the Greek gods had all hankered after humans and made many semidivine beings. If this is the case, it changes nothing, but for giving Moses even more authority.

2) Why does God talk about himself in the third person? Is it because Moses needs enough distance from God to underline his utter subjection to his Word?

Unnumbered observations:

Moses' retirement sets the precedent for graceful yielding of power. There is no democracy to force Moses to yield to Joshua. Only God can force the succession. Later in history, one breathes a little easier when God gives up this job. Democracy relieved God of some of his burdens.

God loves to kill for the ones he loves. "He will wipe out those nations from your path and you shall dispossess them." That sounds like a lot of fun, God, and if that's what you want. . . . In exchange God asks only that he be not ignored or forgotten. However, he knows well that these people for whose sake he had wiped out multitudes will grow fat and forgetful. He knows that they will be bad and that he will punish them. He could *force* them to be good, but he doesn't: he gives them freedom of choice. Why? Is it because he loves to punish them?

Or is it because the Devil, fallen angel that he is, is already preparing the future when he will become an alternative to God, thus giving people a choice but not *freedom* of choice? Is the Devil one of God's inventions gone awry? A story that is going to tell itself, a story that has escaped the authority of the narrator?

Moses' will, God's poem: Moses intends God's poem to be revealed after his death. This poem is Moses' last will: he bequeaths it, within the ark, to the people. Every seven years they will read his will out loud and be reprimanded and rejoined with the Word. Moses' last will was written by God, but it is nonetheless a testamentary document bearing his name.

What is this poem? It's a praise of God himself. It's a mirror. God praises God. Still, God has to pass this mirror on to his people because it's better if *they* praise him. Once more, it seems that God is lonely. He needs company, he needs Moses, he needs the people to read his own words back to him. He needs to speak of himself in the third person. There may not even be any Moses or any people: there may just be God speaking himself through the media of these fictions, these projections of himself that he chooses to call

Moses, people, etc. In any case, it appears that either Moses made up God, in which case God exists only as long as people believe Moses, or God made up Moses, in which case Moses and the people do not exist.

God's fictions present a problem for him: As long as they are part of himself, they have no substance to engage him with. They bore him. In order for them to acquire substance he must feed them milk and honey and fatten them up. This flesh-producing food corrupts them and makes them forgetful. When they begin to forget their creator, his fictions become interesting to God. Perhaps *only* when they forget him do they engage his attention in the general direction of the purpose for which he has created them. So he feeds them milk and honey, which corrupts them, and brings them to a Promised Land, so he can keep his eye on them. Of course, this milk and honey and this Promised Land are conditional upon their worship, not at all like the original paradise, which was eternal (and boring). God, who is eternal, hates eternity because it's boring, so he creates temporal paradises contingent on proper respect.

So, you think it's easy being his creation? Better that Moses made him up. After all, he was only a writer. Like some of us. The poem is not great, but I fault the translation. This poem was supposed to put into words everything that God wanted his people to worship him with, but obviously he did not have translation in mind. Moses' translation was the only one God counted on, but since then there have been a myriad translations into many languages, and something leaked away every time. Which brings up another question: if God wanted his poem forever powerful, why allow its distribution and distortion? Once again, he gives the people free choice: Keep the meaning of this poem or suffer loss.

In addition to being a mirror, this poem is also morality. This poem gives the people the essentials of Good and Bad. Good is to remember and praise God, Bad is to forget him. To put muscle on these notions, Bad is punished, while Good is rewarded (maybe). Of course, the people confuse these notions quite frequently, so the Laws (also written by God and translated by Moses or vice versa) have to back up the distinctions. The Devil, though still quite nameless, is fully present at the succession from nomad time to historical time in the form of amnesia. The Devil is an opiate, pure forgetfulness.

Modern Attitudes and Masques

GOOD NEWS

Pope John Paul II announced that during the year 2000, people who quit smoking or drinking for even one day will get indulgences that will shorten their time in purgatory. This is good news at first, until you think about it. There won't really be that many smokers and drinkers in purgatory because the majority of them are going to hell. Not because they smoke and drink, but because smoking and drinking are usually only part of a sin bundle that's bound to have a lot of other grievous sins wrapped up in it. Unless I'm misreading this, and what the pope is really saying is that there is no hell. He mentions no time off from hell. There hasn't been much talk of purgatory, or indulgences for that matter, since the Council of Trent in 1563. Martin Luther got himself excommunicated for protesting the business of indulgences. Other theologians questioned the whole notion of purgatory and advanced, albeit timidly, the idea that this life we are living right now is in fact purgatory. Beyond that is either paradise or hell. Other radicals, who were happily expunged from the Church even before the Council of Trent, maintained that this life is all three in one, depending on how much God you have in you. These people were called Gnostics, and most of them were burned alive or put to the sword by the pope's armies.

I have no idea what it's like to be pope, or even infallible, but it must be nice to be able to give so much joy to your followers with news of an amnesty. The present pope, who has at times worked in a coal mine, written poetry, overthrown the communists in Poland, got shot at, and kissed Fidel Castro, is no slouch when it comes to worldly strife. And he's no wimp when it comes to church doctrine, either: he won't wink at birth control, he won't let priests marry or women become priests—and now he reaffirms purgatory and the dispensing of indulgences. He's got a firm grip on both worlds, this one and the next.

The only thing the pope doesn't have such a firm grip on is pagans, who keep acting as if there was no pope. A friend of mine writes that for my saint's day I have to rub my door, the doorknob, and the window frames with garlic, and I have to sleep with a garlic clove under my pillow. Next day, I have to put some wheat grains in a dish with water and let them sprout until the Epiphany. I will be as prosperous as the sprouts. Now, this may sound Christian to some people, but it's pure paganism. There is only a short step from such advice to the deliberate practice of witchcraft, wicca-craft, voodoo, Santeria, fire dancing, oriental body twisting and breathing, sword swallowing, all-night dancing, oracle spouting, entrail reading, fetishism, interpretive art, threesomes, and table turning.

For most of us secular wretches, such notions as purgatory have the arresting effect of an incense stick in a slaughterhouse. Sure, it's nice to get time off from the slums just outside the gates of paradise, but meanwhile famine, terror, murder, and torture go on. To his credit, the pope also gave indulgence to anyone who alleviates the suffering of others for even one day. Those who do this can keep on blowing smoke.

Approaches to the Soul

W hat's better for your soul: silence or rock and roll? The Mormons have one answer, the Catholics another.

A recent edict from the Mormon Church has banned e-mail and faxes as ways for its missionaries to communicate with families and friends back home. Young Mormons between the ages of nineteen and twenty-two go on two-year missions to recruit for the Church. Some people have called this communication ban cruel, coming as it did on top of the fact that the young missionaries can only phone home twice a year, on Christmas and Mother's Day, and are only allowed to write one letter a week.

At the same time, a dispatch from Rhode Island says, "Catholic officials are looking for new priests . . . on MTV and cyberspace. Hoping to boost recruitment, the Roman Catholic Diocese of Providence has begun running ads on the cable music network and created a Web site (www.catholic-priest.com)."

Well, here is the difference between a recent cult and an old religion.

The Mormons are strictly patriarchal and, until now, they've had an unshakeable belief in the moral fortitude of their young people. There was no mollycoddling, nor was there any fear of the outside world. The Mormons wanted their young to think for themselves (after brainwashing them real good before they left), and so they cut them off for a while with nothing but the Book of Mormon and their hormones to guide them. What Mormons did with their hormones is not very well known, but it's a safe bet that they battled them in silence. (They probably swatted them with the Book). What is certain is that their temporary banishment gave them a tough handle on their souls. It's probably no accident that the FBI used to recruit mostly Mormons.

But now, the new communication technologies have made leaving home a nonevent. You can stay so plugged in, you'll hardly know you're somewhere else. It's easy to avoid the tough discipline and soul-searching meant to turn an adolescent into a responsible community member. The Mormons won't have it, and I have to admire their resolve.

Such stern soul-shaping goes against the grain of American society now, when adolescence lasts until about the age of fifty. Most young Americans stay kind of unfinished for a very long time, with their identities tied to advertising and entertainment. You'd think that they would be happy in the Garden of Consumerism, but they are not: they are angry and pissed at something vague, as if expecting God (or the Economy) to banish them any minute now. They suspect that something stole their souls and that suspicion is all over their music and Web sites.

The Catholic Church is acknowledging this shaky state of the world and the fact that the young are in limbo. In going to MTV, the Church is recognizing also the desperate spiritual quality of much popular music. There is so much anguish, millennialism, and symbolism jumbled in pop culture, it is fertile ground for recruitment.

The Catholic Church has always accommodated the world just the way it found it, skillfully wrapping its beliefs around people's habits and styles. Most Catholic holidays occur on the dates of older pagan holidays. Pre-Catholic beliefs were rarely obliterated by missionaries, with the notable exceptions of meso-American cultures, which were done in with exceptional brutality. And the Inquisition was no picnic, either. But for all that, the Church has always had a keen eye on the ethos of the masses and on technologies of mass distribution. Rebellious factions within the Church have even sided militantly with the wretched of the earth, claiming souls for social activism before God (who gets the side benefits, in any case). Communication is the soul of activism.

The Mormons just want to stay Mormons, even if it takes recruiting the dead to swell their ranks. (They tried retroactively converting Jews, but they gave up under protest.) There is no e-mailing the dead—yet. The Catholic Church wants everybody to be Catholic and is (pragmatically) sticking to the living, even if they have to pluck them from morally ambiguous cyberspace.

Elvis 20/20: Concluding Remarks at the Third International Elvis Conference in Memphis, Tennessee, 1997

ELVIS=LIVES=EVILS

The fifty-three Australian Elvis fans on Northwest Flight 52 from New Orleans to Memphis, wearing white shirts that said: MEMORIES STILL PLENTY/EVEN AFTER 20/AUSSIE FANS REMEMBER, had no idea that the crew on Flight 52 would run out of Elvis Pepsi cans halfway through the flight! They had no idea that half of the group would never get to carry back to the Australian continent the commemorative cans that said around the rim: STILL ROCKING ELVIS 20 YEARS, and down farther around the picture of the King, PRESLEY'S MEMPHIS — 126 BEALE STREET: UNPRECEDENTED ENTERTAINMENT & CONTEMPORARY CUISINE. WWW.ELVISPRESLEY.COM. INSPIRED BY THE KING OF ROCK 'N' ROLL: ELVIS AND ELVIS PRESLEY ARE REGISTERED TRADEMARKS OF ELVIS PRESLEY ENTERPRISES. VISIT PEPSI WORLD ON THE INTERNET.

This isn't the first time we find Pepsi at the cutting edge. In 1965 in a small communist country behind the Iron Curtain, I read a typewritten poem by Allen Ginsberg, in translation. It said in this poem, "You're in the Pepsi generation." One year later, when I emigrated to New York, I saw this in a subway in three-foot letters: YOU'RE IN THE PEPSI GENERATION. What a grand country, I thought, they are quoting the poets on the walls! One year later, my teacher in things American, Ted Berrigan, pulled me aside and said proudly: "I am the first American poet to put Pepsi in a poem!" Ted drank a lot of it. It probably killed him. I didn't have the heart to say that Allen did it first. Or maybe he didn't, I don't know.

Around the same time Allen Ginsberg was putting Pepsi in his poetry, my Australian seatmate had heard "Heartbreak Hotel," and then, as she put it, "I had to get married next day."

She had to. Dig it. Elvis gave millions of women around the globe their first orgasm, the reverberations or aftershocks of which are still with us. Their fidelity forty years later testifies to the magnitude of the earthquake and, as Douglas Brinkley put it, the coming groundswell of the sixties. In fact, had my Aussie seatmate been ten years younger she might have gotten her first orgasm from Jimi Hendrix and would have found it unnecessary to get married the very next day. So, yes, Elvis did that thing by saying "It's all right, mama," but then most of the girls *did* get married. Eisenhower world was all shook up but it didn't fold. Ten years made a lot of difference to Elvis and to America: He was so startled by what he'd wrought that he wrapped himself in the American flag when he heard that hippies were making love on it.

What the Aussie fans did not know was that, in addition to the lamentable dearth of Pepsi cans on Northwest Flight 52, they were traveling to Memphis with a professor going to the third annual International Elvis Conference at the Memphis College of Art. Had my seatmate known, she might have felt that small pang—like a needle through the eye—that feels like nothing at the time but a few moments later, bang, there is a huge loss. Her Elvis, the people's Elvis, was being taken over by academics and theologians.

At the Memphis College of Art during the Elvis conference, two representatives of the people's Church of Elvis, a modest congregation of fans headquartered on the Internet, demanded the removal of two paintings in the exhibit downstairs. One of them was a representation of Elvis sans loincloth, feeding greedily at the Pamela Anderson–like breast of a saucy madonna. The other was also a Christlike representation of the King crucified sans cloth. The organizers of the conference accommodated the protesters and removed the pictures. Bravo, and good for the humble reps! Had this been some seriously secular-humanist dwelling, they might have had to bring with them their fellow Christian fundamentalist kin and start praying on the steps. As it was, their predicament was well understood and the madonna holding the Christ-child Elvis and the crucified hunk in the other picture were repudiated. The crucified hunk was rather well hung, which brings up the rather interesting question of Elvis's penis. At a time when America's national imagination was filled with penises—including that of the president—Elvis's penis, Elvis's sacred penis found itself repudiated by the very people to whom it, through gyrations and writhings, granted liberatory orgasms in 1957.

It's a knot of mystery. We have, on the one hand, a sexualized generation that has grown old and conservative and which has emasculated its liberator. On the other hand, we have a younger, liberal theological-scholastic institution that is hosting a conference dedicated for the most part, if I heard right, to restoring the scepter to the King. Yet this latter camp feels so unsure about the depth of its faith—whether in art or in its subject—as to cave in to the revisionists. Is this an art issue or a religious one?

Well, it is neither. It is a case of agreement. The job of institutions, notwithstanding the hopeful scholars, is to emasculate God, in whom they don't have much faith anyway. So the aims of the pious Elvinists and the Memphis Art theologians coincide in the end, no matter what their class differences. The two groups have the same aim: to deprive Elvis of his penis. The very material of both institutions is composed of God's chopped-up penis. Lest you think that this is an idle metaphor, let me remind you that Napoleon's penis was sold at auction in London in the nineteenth century and was bought by an English collector who cooked it and ate it. This was no mere English grudge-gourmandise but a concrete ritual of empowerment.

Of course, Elvis himself had offered his penis to the masses, who used it to sexually empower themselves. By so doing, he divested himself of it and became something else, a transformed being who had no choice but to become a gender-ambiguous icon. An Elvis without a penis is a saint—and the tabloids aren't shy in saying so. The elasticity of gender, indeed!

And once again, lest you think me fanciful, I saw a concrete instance of it myself. Patti Carroll, bless her heart, took me into the Elvis impersonator world, a worldwide competition taking place in conjunction with the conference. One particular Elvis impersonator was a wheelchair Elvis, a handicapped Elvis with a beautiful voice. He was paralyzed from the waist down, having no practical use of the very part that made Elvis Elvis. The audience applauded him heartily in the generous spirit of the nineties, just as they had applauded, wildly, an impersonator from Japan. So Elvis impersonators and their fans have reached a level of understanding of their craft, which involves parody, tolerance, and quite a distancing from the source.

The Elvis impersonators' audience was composed in equal parts of self-consciousness and nostalgia. For some of the older folk present, the impersonators were the Doors of Meat which led to their past. They hurled themselves relentlessly against these Doors of Meat, hoping to dislodge them and return to paradise. The younger audience self-consciously appreciated the campiness of it all.

Now, clearly, the fundamentalists who succeeded doing away with the art here do not have the degree of self-consciousness or good humor of the impersonators' audience. Or perhaps it is just a matter of degree. I have ascertained, on the basis of first- and secondhand reports, that, from the point of view of the principals, it was an *Elvis* issue, not a God issue. That is, the people who wanted the pictures removed thought that they were an insult to Elvis, and the people who removed them thought that might be true. Which makes it an Elvis issue for everyone involved except for the artists who thought that the separation of church and state in this country is real. I believe that for the artists it is an economic issue: The people who allowed their pictures to be removed were not very good competitors in the marketplace because they folded before the agents of fundamentalist Elvis kitsch.

But enough of this. I have been told, by other shaky liberal humanists, to stay away from eschatology, so I will. I will say only one more thing about it and then move on to other issues. When the Christian God exploded at the end of the nineteenth century, his shards landed and continue to land on fourteen-year-old prepubescents. I have no doubt that one of these landed on Elvis—and he was created from that Big Bang. When Elvis himself exploded, a number of shards landed all over the place, entering hundreds of impersonators and others. We can call this second Big Bang the Gang Bang. This mystery continues to generate more and more Elvis all the time at an increasing rate. Eventually the whole world will be Elvis.

When I first got to Memphis, I walked from the Peabody Hotel to the Memphis College of Art on Poplar Avenue. I walked past the county jail, the juvenile detention hall, ten bail bondsmen, fenced-in vacant lots, the boarded up Tri-State Liquor, six pawn shops, one psychiatric hospital/prison, two halfway houses, the Alcohol Drug & Treatment Center, the AIDS-Support Services headquarters, two very unsettling housing projects, and the most lively business, something called Joe Gins, advertising CANA-DIAN HIGH TEN MILE. Not an Elvis in sight, but surely a place for the blues. I had the vision that Jesus himself did in fact sing his parables. The music was lost. Still, there wasn't a taxi or an Elvis in sight on Poplar that Sunday—they were all at Graceland or at the Memphis Museum of Art or being interviewed.

Which brings me to El Vez, the Mexican Elvis, whose hip appropriation of Elvis music to the cause of the downtrodden was well analyzed at the conference. I like El Vez because he really rocks and has a good voice, but I can't say that I'm so crazy about his message-lyrics. There is an authoritarian cast to them. Their radicalism is only subversive in the white world of Elvis fans. If I were one of the subjects of his lyrics, I'd feel condescended to—like, do I really need to get my Chicano Pride 101 from rock 'n' roll? I would demand more mystery, more detail, less sloganeering. This is just carping, though, because in the world of infinite white Elvises, El Vez's activity is quite Christ-like. He is not so much an Elvis devotee as an Elvis competitor, the Antichrist.

The academic Elvis we've been setting up here all week, the meta-Elvis, the all-encompassing, revolutionary Elvis, the subsuming Elvis, is also the Antichrist. Many brilliant comments have been made for the purpose of restoring the "real Elvis" from the rumbling belly of consumer culture where he's been more than half digested, sequins and all. Some of us feel that the postmortem Elvis metastasis has nearly obliterated an American revolutionary. We are attempting to cleanse, purify, and restore a precise Elvis for classroom use. However, I am afraid that this Elvis is just another in a long series of postmortem Elvises.

Several things mattered to *me*, significantly, that week. Foremost was the music. I always liked Elvis songs, but I was too late to feel orgasmic about any of it. Hearing the songs there, contextualized by all this fever and color, I really, really dug them. Second, I gained a healthy respect for both the historical Elvis and the phenomena he represents. I mean respect in the sense that provocative ideas were generated, worthy of further reflection. I particularly like Professor Vernon Chadwick's notion of "trans-cultural localism," because as a trans-cultured Southerner, I feel included. If the conference was about liberating Elvis the liberator from the tabloids, it was quite successful. I was equally interested, however, in the impersonators' contest, where the pathos of aging in America was brought to me more forcefully than at our academic discussions. I saw the whole vast vistas of face-lifts, the palliatives of Las Vegas, the fidelity to that first orgasm stretch into the future like the mega-retirement communities of Florida and Arizona. Watching the grandmas throw themselves at the sweating gyrating hunks, hoping to break down the Doors of Meat to the past, is enough to make me cry.

In the end, Elvis is a kind of measuring device, an E-meter that registers class, age, and humor in America. One of our chief sources of cultural torment in this country is the fake class distinctions brought about by consumerism. The relentless production of ersatz goods attempts to fool the working poor into thinking that they live just like the rich: The stuff looks the same, even though it's Naugahyde instead of natural fiber. Until, of course, Naugahyde acquires chic value, and then the poor have to go to the next ersatz level. The E-meter is a palimpsest of images: the original is working-class Southern white trash and the Liberator, then there is Elvis (still living) parodying himself pathetically in a simulacrum of patriotism, the ersatz Elvis of Vegas, and then come all the high and low postmortem Elvises. Incidentally, Patti Carroll introduced me to a Mrs. Hunt who lives in Rome and has discovered, in a well-known Giotto fresco, a pre-Elvis masquerading as St. Francis. So there is that.

I will end this by revealing to you the contents of a note found by a friend of a friend in Elvis's wastebasket, shortly before he died. He gave me this note because he trusted my academic credentials and knew that I'd be going to the conference. The note says: "Give me a break." That's all. "Give me a break." I think we have done that, literally: broken off another Elvis from the Elvis tree. "Give me a break." Yeah, right. Elvis, you're not in charge. You never were.

The Millennium Pics

Here is a typical Midwestern family waiting for Y2K: large mom and dad and five chunky offspring, all holding shotguns and pistols before a mound of Ramen soups, Campbell's soup cans, cracker boxes, and condensed milk. "We are ready," they tell the reporter, and you can see that they are. You try to get close to that Ramen, buddy, and your brains will be all over the cornfield.

The people in this magazine pic, like tens of thousands of other determined survivalists, are stocking up on dry and canned goods all over the North American continent, happy that, finally, they can show the world that they are *somebody*, that come what may, their determined overweight family unit will outlast the millennium glitch.

It's a new craze, but the urge to be self-sufficient, shoot intruders, and become the stuff of legends is as old as the Puritans and at least as old as Hollywood. The Western drive was all about dry food and rifles and surviving the Indians, who were the main glitch back then. The only difference is that the Indians were real and the food wasn't radiated for longevity. Back then, you rarely posed for magazines because there was no time.

The new survivalists have barely mastered the basics of the computers they fear will end their world. People in Third World countries, who never even saw computers, have no idea what the fuss is all about. If the electricity fails, as it does every other day, they light candles or go out and look at the moon. If they want to eat, they dig something out of the garden or eat somebody's family pet. If banks fail, they take cash out of the mattress and pay somebody to fix the well. If airplanes fall out of the sky, they look for nice debris. None of their kin were on board.

At the same time that countless Americans are readying themselves to put up armed resistance against Ramen raiders, other countless Americans are hoping to have a baby on the stroke of midnight 2000. The winner of the timeliest millennium baby gets all kinds of unspecified perks and a life-time of something to talk about.

Now, here is another picture: the baby is coming, the hospital staff and visitors are cheering, the countdown to the New Year has started and . . . the Y2K glitch kicks in. All the lights go out, everybody starts screaming, the baby pushes out into the darkness. The hospital generator kicks in and, in the flickering light, the distraught padre bites off the umbilical cord. The baby is held aloft and a battery-operated camera flashes. It's in the newspa-pers next day.

Meanwhile, in the Midwest, the family has been firing into the dark be-cause they thought they'd heard something. They had. It was the new mil-lennium, laughing at them. And they keep firing at it.

Human Remedies Against the Devil

Cemeteries are reassuring: they provide continuity. The dearly departed do not need as much room as they used to, but they still have an address. They are available twenty-four hours a day in any weather. There may be fog draping their little house or a downpour trying to drown it, but invariably the occupants are home. This may be small comfort to the widow who never could keep the living husband home, but it's a promissory note that things will be different in heaven. Catholic tombstones are waiting rooms for the Day of Judgment. In their little perennial houses, the dead rehearse their defense for the Almighty and rest for the day when they will be called to rise and utilize their creaky bodies again. The cities of the dead are busy places, but like cities of the living, their character varies. And the souls, of course, do not stay put. They voyage.

New Orleans cemeteries are like New Orleans: They swing between destitution and opulence but always with style. Even the humblest marker in potter's field projects something native: The pathos of scrawled names and the black bordered cross rhymes with the willow and the mossy oak in the cloudy sky. The mightiest marble in the Metairie Cemetery says no more than this, though loudly instead of whispering. The dead in New Orleans are interred above the muddy gumbo of the soil to keep them from slipping away in the water. The dead are drier than the living, and that accounts for their air of superiority. They have shelter, eternity, and are cautiously but faithfully attended by the living. They are also more numerous than the living—the reward of an old city—and love to congregate, haunt, and dance. Only the thinnest film, a razor-edge of twilight, separates them from their descendants. The clouds are no mere romantic props but portents and soul carriers. They drift over the graves, ghostly tour boats from which the dead view their own abodes as well as the living.

On All Saints' Day in the city of New Orleans, the kin of the departed gather in cemeteries to clean the tombs, wipe the grime of late-twentieth-century air, brush away oak leaves, uproot impertinent banana trees, pick off cigarette butts and used syringes, and scrub clean the graffiti that, like a new force of nature, besets even the noblest. The keepers of the graves are mostly old women these days, who remember their *mamère* and *papère* and *granmère* and *grampère*. Their own resting places await them in the family crypts. To make room, the oldest bones are lowered into a pit at the bottom so that the recently dead are assured a berth until they too are displaced by another generation. Long before the actual passing, great care is taken in deciding which berth one will lie on. Ending up next to a disliked relative can sour eternity. The grave keepers listen to the bones, remember, plot, pray, and scrub.

The first dead were, of course, the Creoles, French and Spanish nobles, who had the misfortune to settle in the fetid swamp from which the city rose. Later Europeans, notably Irish and German peasants, died of yellow fever and cholera. Some of the nobles perished young, and when their epitaphs contain the word *honor,* it usually means that they were killed in a duel. The scions of colonial nobility carried the manners of old Europe all the way to their graves, but the occasion for the duels belonged wholly to the New World. At St. Louis No. 1 Cemetery, for instance, there is one Louis Philogene Duclos, whose stone proclaims, "*Ci gît Louis Duclos, ensigne dans les Troupes des États de l'Amérique, fils légitime de Rodolphe Joseph Duclos et de Marie Lucie de Reggi. Né le 18 Août 1791, décédé le 4 Juillet 1811.*" Louis died before the War of 1812, so it isn't quite clear to which United States troop he belonged, but one thing is very clear: the word *légitime* means that he was the result of a liaison between a French Creole and a quadroon mistress. We will never know if Louis was recognized before he died, but in the end he was brought into the bosom of the family. Creole men had quadroon and octoroon mistresses whose offspring were occasionally admitted to the family tomb, though never to the family table. The neighborhood where these women lived, in pretty cottages smothered in jasmine and draped in weeping willows, still stands. Their graves are less easily found. Louis's mother lies shrouded in anonymity, though one might easily imagine Louis's father defending her honor in a duel. The complexities of love, lust, honor, and skin color swirl in a fine mist around the gravestones of New Orleans.

Those mythic beginnings, still visible in the oldest cemeteries, like St. Louis No. 1, translated into yet more extravagant complexities later. At the close of the nineteenth century and the beginning of the twentieth, New Orleans became North America's pleasure dome. Out of its fleshpots rose jazz, America's music. The institution of the mistress was reaffirmed and some of the later mistresses were not to be trifled with even in death. Josie Arlington was a notorious *fille de joie* who carefully designed her tomb at the Metairie Cemetery to tower over the more modest resting place of her married lover and his legitimate wife. Josie's image struck two flambeaux on each side to project a rose light that made it seem as if she haunted the place. It is a sad fact that all flesh must die, but there is no reason why one's story, as well as one's soul, should be slighted after the passage. The attraction artists feel for our cemeteries is only partly aesthetic; much of it is gossip, a continual whisper intended for the delighted ear. Marble without a story is just marble. A true monument leans over and murmurs in your ear.

The graves of New Orleans follow social standing, just like their residents had. I have not looked rigorously into the distribution of angels, but I assume that they were commissioned by the wealthy. Marching past St. Roch Cemetery one time around twilight, with a group of antifascist protesters, I was struck by the proliferation of angels massed in the sky. They were in flight, taking off toward each other, as animated as large winged creatures ever get. Their milky white flesh glowed, their robes came undone, the flowers they held glistened, their hair was on fire. David Duke, the racist against whom we were marching, was defeated the next day. Miracles are very much part of St. Roch: look at the prosthetic limbs left by the faithful in the St. Roch chapel. They were healed and made strong enough to march against racists. Well, maybe. Faith may have no politics, but it does seem to belong disproportionately to the poor. Which makes it all the more fair to employ the angels of the rich to the purposes of justice.

The majority of the tombstones of New Orleans are *sans anges*: they resemble baking ovens. They are called "burial ovens," in fact, and one might easily imagine the dead, laid out like loaves of bread, baking quietly in the sun. Perhaps when they are crisp like the baguettes at La Madeleine, they are allowed to leave their graves and frolic with the rest. "We bake in purgatory," Dante said, "before we are set on the Table of Judgment, / sure to hear our story again."*

Some tombs are made from the remains of other tombs, whose owners have vanished. In 1866, the famous Théâtre d'Orléans, which had amused the Creoles for decades, burned down, and its bricks were bought by the owner of the Louisa Street Cemetery who made them into burial ovens. It might not seem so unusual then to hear someone say, as I did, that New Orleans cemeteries "sing at night." Of course they do, and this is why people sing even louder: to drown out the dead. Any given night on Rampart Street you can audit the competition: the singers and bands making merry at the Funky Butt are barely rising above the din of dead choruses and howling cats across the street at St. Louis No. 1.

New Orleans cemeteries sing at night, but they are pretty quiet in the morning when I take my coffee there. I started using places of eternal rest for my private coffeehouses way back in my adolescence, when getting away from the horrible noises of adults was a necessity. In my hometown of Sibiu, in Transylvania, Romania, there was a German Catholic cemetery that was as angel-rife and ornate as any in New Orleans. I wrote poetry there among listing urns and reposing burghers, and dreamt of the day when I would take a girl there to show her my favorite inscriptions. That day came soon enough, and I surrendered my virginity to our resident junior-high nymph, Marinella, on the grave of one Herr Titus Bruckenthal who'd been, if memory serves right, a candlemaker. When I first moved to New Orleans, I was overjoyed to be living within walking distance of Lafayette Cemetery, which has a fair number of Germans baking in it. The Lafayette Cemetery also sits kitty-corner from the apartment house where F. Scott Fitzgerald, age 23, is rumored to have begun his first novel, *This Side of Paradise*. From his window, Scotty, possibly hungover on Prohibition gin, would have had a pretty good view of the tombstones in the Lafayette. "All right," he might have addressed the entombed, "it ain't so hot on *this* side of paradise."

I once took a Polish artist, Krystof, to the Lafayette for a cup of coffee. We

---

*Dante Alighieri, *The Divine Comedy*, unpublished translation by A. Codrescu.

sat on the funeral slab of a certain Tadeusz Millhauser, and he told me that he led a student strike in Warsaw during the late days of communism. He had taken his fellow students to the old Warsaw cemetery, and together they had studied true Polish history from tombstones, a history very unlike the lies told in the propaganda textbooks of their schools. The dead listened carefully, taking notes for their nightly meets. I wouldn't be surprised if Krystof's story became a song that traveled throughout the world of the dead and was instrumental in bringing down the Berlin Wall a few weeks later. A footnote was that I took Krystoff to Commander's Palace across the street from the cemetery and they told us that they were booked until I explained that my friend was Václav Havel, the future president of Czechoslovakia. The dead in New Orleans, in addition to singing, pay for stories with restaurant reservations.

A certain dead waiter at Antoine's, one of the city's grand restaurants, caused quite a problem when he died without designating a successor. The way a rabbi from New Jersey put it, "I lived in New Orleans for five years and I finally got my own waiter at Antoine's. Then he died, and I moved. I had no idea how to get another waiter. Mine came to me from a blue-blooded New Orleanian, who bequeathed him to me when he had to move to Paris to take care of his dying sister." Waiting tables at Antoine's is in itself a hereditary position, passed on from father to son. A true New Orleans blue blood must have a waiter as well as a tombstone, and a waiter must have a true blue-blooded client as well as a tombstone. For myself, the pleasure of eating in an old restaurant is intimately linked to the comfort of death. "Ah," I think to myself at Antoine's, or Commander's Palace, or any of the grand establishments, "One hundred years ago a man sat where I sit now, had a fine meal, and died." This makes me inexpressibly happy. I feel that my pleasure is authorized by continuity, that it is not ephemeral the way it is in all those horrid, brand-spanking-new, automobile-riddled, and soulless clusters that pass for cities in America.

I have visited dead poets in famous cemeteries and found them at work. In the Protestant cemetery in Rome John Keats lies under a tombstone that does not bear his name. "This grave contains all that was mortal of a YOUNG ENGLISH POET who on his death bed in the Bitterness of his Heart at the Malicious Power of his Enemies, Desired These Words to be Engraven on his Tombstone: Here Lies One Whose Name is Writ in Water. February 24th 1821." A lyre-shaped tree shadows the grave and shelters the cats of Rome, who love these grounds. Walt Whitman planned his monument, which rests in Camden, New Jersey, in a circular grove of oaks. The tomb cost Whitman more than his house. On the grave of Guillaume Apollinaire in the Père Lachaise Cemetery in Paris there is a poem in the shape of an up-side-down heart made from the words: MON COEUR PAREIL A UNE FLAMME RENVERSÉE (My Heart Like an Upside-Down Flame).

Tombstones are essential tools of poetry. I am not speaking only of the tombstones of poets, which are of course professional tools, but all tombstones. New Orleans cemeteries are among the most poetic I have ever visited. They are a mother lode for poets, and I have taken my students to them on many an occasion. Cemeteries bring out the storytellers in people. My friend James Nolan, a New Orleans–born poet who lived for many years in Spain and San Francisco, returned here and began writing stories about his family tomb. In New Orleans, he told me, the dead lead an active afterlife. They are invoked frequently, remembered often, and sometimes *seen*. More important, they speak to the living and aren't really shy about it.

The voodoo religion, which is a mix of African worship and Catholic rite, takes the dead very seriously. Offerings are made at gravesites, and the dead are addressed with the greatest respect. The tomb of Marie Laveau, the so-called Voodoo Queen who popularized this practice in the late nineteenth century, is often festooned with charred bones, half- empty glasses of rum, cigars that have been a little smoked, coins, feathers, and prayer-poems. In the French Quarter courtyard of one of my friends, a stone voodoo shrine is mysteriously attended every full moon. The worshippers leave behind offerings, but my friend has never been able to see them, though he has waited and watched.

It is important that one get to one's final resting place in vivid and memorable fashion. In New Orleans, the jazz funerals of important members of the black community are shining models of respect and remembrance. The deceased is seen off by musical bands, followed by dancing friends, acquaintances, and strangers. The throng sways under twirling yellow and black umbrellas, accompanying the deceased as near to the next world as it is possible for the living. Surely, by showing their affection in this way, they now have a friend in the next world. I once followed such a procession, without a clue as to who the departed was, and when we got to the cemetery, a man told us, "You have one trumpet on your side when you go." It turned out the man was a trumpeter. I don't have my own waiter at Antoine's, but I have a trumpet in heaven.

Another Autumn

Niciodata nu fu toamna mai frumoasă
sufletului nostru doritor de moarte.

Autumn was never this splendid
to our death-thirsty soul.

—Tudor Arghezi

Here it is, the rich golden light that announces for the umpteenth time that it's autumn in the world, with its smell of apples and chalk. A new urgency grips the young, an old guilt spurs on the lassitude-heavy bodies of summer. We are all hurtling toward the millennium, resolved to make a difference, to make sense, to produce something. This autumn we will invent something greater than the spork—though it's hard to imagine anything greater than that. Will we say, "We have come to a spork in the road?" or, "He was born with a silver spork in his mouth?" Probably not, but our new inventions will certainly attempt it. After the losses of each year, there seems to be more room in the world, there are voids everywhere.

Nineteen ninety-seven was a particularly grievous year. Many giants of American poetry are gone: Ginsberg, Burroughs, Jim Gustafson, Gerald Burns. Gone too are many mad children of the sixties, Heaven's Gaters all, led like a flock of psychedelic geese by Timothy Leary, destination Comet Hale-Bopp. And closely behind them in the luminous void, the young British princess and the saint of lepers, all of them swept up by the ill winds of 1997. I remember only one year worse than that one, the year 1977, when some of my dearest friends were plucked in the flower of their youth. Is there something about seven, that number Europeans cross at the waist with a line, as if cancelling something? Is there something about the summers of years with the number seven in them? Numerologists may know something, but all I know is that fall narrows like a wind tunnel and the end of the year is in sight. If we come out of it, we should meet the new exigencies of the future, their faces veiled, their shapes unknown, their mysteries more promising and terrifying than ever. The future always lies in the womb of autumn—the inevitable fruit of loss and promise. But hard like a seed in the flesh of it is the bitterness of this year. And it was bitter.

To: James Grauerholz
    Jim McCrary

Dear Ones:

Pass the word to WILLIAM that there is a huge hole on this prison-planet now that he's joined his friends on the next level. My condolences to you. I imagine you'll be swamped with memorials & regrets for the next year so I won't make this too long. One thing's for sure: William Burroughs won't go to any Christian outfit. He's straight up in the Buddha-place with Ginzy & Jack.

Andrei Codrescu
New Orleans
August 2, 1997

To: Allen Ginsberg
    Naropa Institute
    Boulder, Colorado

November 1, 1993

Dear Allen,

I have been pursuing your fleet form through lo these many months through many lands because we need you desperately! We (*Exquisite Corpse* staff) are going to publish an anthology called *American Poets Say Goodbye to the 20th Century.** We need your long or short goodbye for our book. The book would be nothing without your goodbye because you are the poet of half this century. I am hoping that you can apply yourself to a millennial meditation for us. This is a call for poems, so naturally, we would prefer something composed in your incomparable first thought key. Failing that, we will take the work short or long that you think is most thematically appropriate. This will be a great book: we have asked one hundred or so of our most distinguished practitioners and they've all said yes. Our deadline is January 1, 1994. Please FAX back: 504-899-4608, to set our uneasy minds at ease. Say yes. The book will be published in the Fall of 1994 by Four Walls/Eight Windows in collaboration with *Exquisite Corpse*. It will be a hefty, rich and inclusive collection that will see the century off with the music it deserves.

I hope that you are happy.

Millennially Yours, With Love,
The *Exquisite Corpse* Editor
Andrei Codrescu

---

*NB: American Poets Say Goodbye to the 20th Century, *edited by Andrei Codrescu and Laura Rosenthal, was published in 1996. It contains Allen Ginsberg's poem "Calm Panic Campaign Promise," which he sent us from New York, and William Burroughs's "Lack."*

Allen Ginsberg

Allen Ginsberg, old courage teacher, is gone. I met Allen in 1966 when I was nineteen years old, fresh out of Romania. I knocked on his door in the Lower East Side in New York and brashly presented my baby-dissident credentials to the President of Poetry. Far from being startled, the poet gave generously of his time and welcomed me to the language, the country, and New York. We spoke French because my English was nonexistent, and he loaded me with books of poetry he thought I should read and study. Always the teacher, always generous, Allen Ginsberg was not only the most famous poet in the world, but the kindest as well. Over the years, it was always a privilege to bask in his light, to revel in the privilege of knowing him, to follow his passions. He was beloved of four generations of American poets, beginning with the one he founded and promoted, right down to the youngest of the young, children my son's age, who love his work more than any other poet's. He inspired rebellion and backed it with the wisdom of the age and the genius of a pacifist, benign, and visionary spirit. He brought us all into a family of great souls that included the Buddhist writers of the sutras, William Blake, and his twin soul, Walt Whitman. Allen Ginsberg was America's best ambassador for the kind of democracy Walt Whitman extolled, and he deplored, cursed, and lamented the failings of public men to live up to that ideal. He lashed out against the wrong-headed war in Vietnam, he deplored the stupid official drug policies of the government, and he lobbied for sexual liberty. He defended the powerless at every turn, and, at the same time, he showed us all how to live without fear, and with joy and courage. Ginsberg believed in the power of poetry and served as mentor and protector of poets outside the mainstream. He founded the Jack Kerouac Institute of Disembodied Poetics at the Naropa Institute in Boulder, Colorado, as an antidote to the establishment that belatedly honored him but denied his comrades and his heirs. He led the charge magnificently, a warm and intimate human being who understood the deep spirituality of the everyday and the long vision of who we are. I am sorry that he did not see the end of a century whose spirit he embodied, but his job is far from done. As long as Allen Ginsberg was alive, we were all sort of immortal. Now we can put away such foolishness, and get on with the poem.

Hello, Cosmos!

THIS FROM MY JOURNAL IN 1997:

The word is Tim Leary is going to kill himself "live" on the Internet, sometime during the next two weeks. You can turn on, tune in, and watch Tim drop out, in real time. You can download his last breath, catch his soul exit his body, witness the passage, all in color if you have a good computer. I'm not sure how I feel about it, but as an artist I can certainly commend him for this first-of-its-kind performance. The new art of Public Self-Snuff is now born, sure to be followed by the Internet Self-Snuff of many lesser luminaries, to be followed in time by public mass suicides. The avant-garde, as we know, always ends up at Wal-Mart sooner or later.

A while ago, I proposed the idea of the Net as an afterlife, which, I theorized, was nature's way of thinning the affluent (who don't die fast enough) with the help of their own toys. There are already cemeteries in cyberspace: now there will be live suicides and burials, too. (The poor will always die like they have, from poverty, diseases, and anonymity.)

Public death is, of course, nothing new. Executions were once public, the favorite entertainment of the rabble. People used to lift children on their shoulders to watch people die. What's new is the potentially vast audience of voyeurs, assisting in the act. Move over, Kevorkian. We can now all be

Kevorkians, ready to assist and abet. It will be a grand party. Some people will, doubtlessly, drop acid and make love, hoping to conceive at the very moment of Tim Leary's death, for a chance his soul will enter the baby. Tim II may arrive before Tim I is properly eulogized.

Whatever Tim's last words, I stand in awe. I remember trying once to read his *Psychedelic Prayers*, in a heightened state. I found them quite humorous. But now, before this great gesture, I stand in awe. Whatever Tim's last words, 'tis pity we'll hear no more his Irish charm and verve. Surely he will make a splendid saint in the Great Bardo. Go, Tim.

April 26, 1996

Timothy Leary did not die live on the Internet, but his head has been cryogenically preserved.

Week of the Dead

Jim Gustafson wrote this in his book of poetry, *Virtue and Annihilation:* "Oh, the dances we have done! The Ballet Diabolique, / The Wonderland One-Step, / The Dipso Calypso . . . / Everywhere we went . . . and we went everywhere / we danced. / Danced until the cows came home / and left / appalled. / We danced to keep from dreaming. / danced to keep from dying / but mostly / we just danced."

On Sunday I went to Jim's funeral in Detroit. My friend Jim Gustafson had danced his last. Jim was a poet and a novelist, bon vivant, raconteur, and legend. He was also my walking pal in San Francisco many years ago: We walked up and down hills, full of youth, poetry, life, and a terrible unfocused hunger for the world. We had no money at all, but we always contrived to find someone willing to buy us drinks. We were a spectacle, aerialists of the spirit. You had to be filled with wonder just to know how to watch us. The world was fresh then, all bud and sap. The sorrow and the dying that would soon overtake so many of our friends had not yet arrived. After San Francisco, Jim lived in Bolinas, Baltimore, and New York, before returning to Detroit, his beloved and scary city about which he once wrote: "Detroit lies there / like the head of a pig on a platter." He called Detroit "Discount City" in one of his novels, and explained his return thus: "He'd run out of faith, explanations, workable teeth, traveler's checks, cohesion, copulating partners and locomotion simultaneously." Still, he found a core of adoring friends at the heart of Motor City, poets, artists, bartenders, and waitresses, who indulged him, admired his wit, and took, sighing, his late-night calls to listen to his latest poem.

Jim would have liked his wake: We told stories and read his new poems. We read his newest new poems which were eerily prescient in describing both the manner and the timing of his death. But then, good poets always know. César Vallejo, the Peruvian, knew that he would die on a rainy day in autumn in Paris. Jim Gustafson, the Detroiter, knew that his own brain would overtake him because it teemed with ideas and was never still. He even named the explosion in a poem: aneurysm. And he spelled it right.

I'll go on telling Gustafson stories for years. Wherever I go there is usually someone who knew him and that is enough to make us light up and remember. Why, there was that time when we walked into the Coffee Gallery in San Francisco's North Beach and signed up to read for the free wine. Trouble was we had no poems with us, so before our turn came we composed ten. And were the toast of the tavern. And then, there was that time when . . .

The Manners of the Unspeakable

W e get older, people we love die, people we love are struck by disease, people we love draw closer in an ever-tightening circle of grief. Dying and illness have a sober set of requirements. How does one say what needs to be said, how does one say *anything*? No book can help you with this, because what you say to a dying friend must come from the heart and what's in your heart is never in books, not even in the best ones.

I saw my friend and former student Matt Clark two nights before he died. He was hooked up to life supports in his own bed with his family around him. His breathing was labored. I couldn't tell if he was conscious or not, but I like to think that he was, that he knew I was there. I kissed his forehead, held his hand, mumbled something about love. I couldn't say, "it's going to be all right," because I knew that it wasn't going to be, and I was no priest who might promise allrightness somewhere else. "Love," it seems to me, is about the only word under the circumstances, but what an awkward word! Matt was young, thirty-two years old. He had worked for me one year, was a promising writer, a man with a sense of humor, and had an extraordinary ambition: He wanted to be a high-school teacher. He was sane, in the best sense of that word. I had certainly liked him, enjoyed his presence, was going to miss him. But "love" was there only in the end, a summary of all those feelings coming together in that single word-gush of sympathy and regret.

Matt was the youngest of those who died recently. The past two years have seen carnage among my contemporaries and my elders. Jim Gustafson. Kathy Acker, one of the bright lights of my young days in San Francisco. Allen Ginsberg, William Burroughs, Jack Micheline, Timothy Leary—*that* generation, all gone at once, in a flock, the way they had often been perceived.

But death may not be the worst thing, after all. Worse than death is the knowledge that corruption has set in, that the creaking machinery of the body that had done so splendidly in love, is now menaced by sudden terrors. People have heart attacks, cancer stuns younger people, or, at least, so it seems from here. I hear this news and my first impulse is to run, to pretend that I didn't hear. I don't want to talk to them—probably because I fear contamination. Death is contagious and greedy. But, of course, I can't. I have to do the grown-up thing, I have to call them, visit them, and assure them of my love, conscious too that I am assuaging my own guilty conscience and very little of their real pain.

Being a grown-up sucks, to coin a phrase.

How Do You Say Goodbye to the 20th Century?

ANOTHER QUESTION OF MANNERS

There are many ways to say goodbye to the twentieth century—at least as many as there are to leave your lover—and I will not enumerate all of them in all the languages I know. You know what happened in California when too many people said, "Have a nice day"—there was a four-year drought.

Most of us will say goodbye the way we said hello. In other words, we won't say anything because we have no choice in the matter. It is usually the parents who say hello when a baby is born, not the other way around. The parents always say a big HELLO when a baby is born, but in the case of those of us, like myself, born just after World War II, our parents said a real BIG HELLO because the war was over. But it wasn't an unambiguous HELLO, it was more like, HELLO, I HOPE YOU WON'T HAVE TO GO THROUGH THE SAME SHIT WE DID.

Well, we didn't—we went through different shit.

Jack Skelley, a poet and reporter from Los Angeles, asked me, how do you say goodbye to the twentieth century, and I told him: You get two hundred poets to say it for you. Laura Rosenthal and I edited an anthology called *American Poets Say Goodbye to the 20th Century*. We asked five hundred poets to write a poem saying goodbye to it: Three hundred of them didn't want to. I don't blame them. I'm superstitious myself and I wouldn't want to say goodbye for fear that the century, in a bad mood, might say goodbye *to me*, before it was all over. In fact, it happened to several poets in our book: Charles Bukowski, Joe Cardarelli, Jim Gustafson, Gerald Burns, Allen Ginsberg, William Burroughs, Tom Dent. James Laughlin, who published the twentieth century, stayed out of it. He died before it was over, anyway. Others simply shied away from the whole idea because it was too porten-tous, maybe too pretentious. Others probably did not believe that there was such a thing as the twentieth century, an arbitrary division of time created for the convenience of historians and anthologizers.

For others yet, the twentieth century was not enough. They had bigger things in mind. Gary Snyder suggested that we call on poets to say their farewells to the millennium. The twentieth century, it seemed to him, was only a speck in the millennial tide and the millennium itself was no more than a blip to the earth, the living entity that sets its clock by rocks and stars.

Carving out a millennium from such duration seems like an exercise in futility. The only millennium we might have anthologized was the Chris-tian one, beginning in original sin and ending in utopia. Not being terribly Christian, we were understandably queasy. But then, for the most part, the millennial perspective was willfully absent from the poetry we received, de-liberately excised in fact.

And when that wasn't the case, it was dissolved in the bath of irony, a na-tive twentieth-century substance. "god's very / possibly way outta here," wrote Jonathan Williams. Faye Kicknosway wrote that "God is a dimwit." And Maxine Kumin wondered, "And what terror awaits those among us / whose moral priorities are unattached / to Yahweh, Allah, Buddha, or Christ?"

It's hard to say adios when God's gone.

The truth is that the twentieth century, the American century, mattered far more to our poets than did the Christian millennium. There were few calls for redemption. On the contrary, there were many refusals of it. Tom Clark asked only (only!) what will become of the "lyric spirit," that "seed of some miraculous plant preserved under the glacial weight of adverse times." Robert Creeley affirmed that in his lifetime, "Yet I loved, I love." And for Edward Field, hope attaches to "poetry, fantasy, weapons for non-fighters."

There is no hint of the Messiah, not one welcoming sign. There are no calls for salvation. On the contrary, these questions and affirmations block, knowingly, the alibi of some Huge Other, whether evil or benign. Embarrassment escorts the end and denial greets the beginning.

The twentieth century is where we have lived our lives. Where we were compelled to embody modern differences. We were constituted to be utterly unlike the centuries that came before us. At times, this was a great hope, all that revolutionary newness in a stale world. Apollinaire and Marinetti, before the First World War, greeted the aesthetics of steel girders and engines. Mayakovski painted the bathos, beauty, and redemptive pull of his communist faith in twenty-foot letters. Such seriousness! Such faith! Likewise Marinetti, embracing a similar though more heinous faith, that of fascism. Happily, there was Mina Loy (who is not in the book) to apply that tonic and bitter irony without which the sorrow would never end: "The door was an absurd thing / Yet it was passable / They quotidienly passed through it / It was this shape / Gina and Miovani / Who they were God knows / They knew / it was important to them / This being who they were / They were themselves / corporeally transcendentally / consecutively / conjunctively and they were quite complete."

Mina and Giovanni—without the ten-foot letters.

Happily and necessarily, irony was in the world. Tristan Tzara could declare, while the utopian machine of the Russian Revolution was being deployed: "I am still charming." Thank God (in whom no one trusts).

Mayakovski, sick of his own grandeur and the lies it authorized, committed suicide. But Tristan Tzara became a communist. And the glamorous and ironic Mina Loy became a bag lady in the Bowery. There were ironies bigger than all of them.

The poetic enterprise of our century's beginnings consisted of attempts to partake of the bounty of forms bequeathed by the future and to humanize the machine. And there were those, happily, who censured both conceits, and put the focus on the daily. Mina Loy, Gertrude Stein, Tristan Tzara, Marcel Duchamp . . . and these are begetters of many of the young and youngish poets in this book. Words like *millennium* make them draw their slingshots. But nobody, neither the begetters nor the begettees, is safe from those bigger ironies that work, it seems, for a stern monolith just below hearing range.

By the 1930s nobody was smiling. What was human had to be defended against what was not: vast warring ideologies, war itself, genocide. The mass graves just behind us had many poets in them. From Max Jacob, who was killed by the Nazis, to Paul Celan, who killed himself later because the Nazis had murdered his parents; from Osip Mandelstam, who was killed by Stalin for a poem, to García Lorca, shot by fascists in Spain—from one gallows tree to another, there is little to smirk about. "Cunning, silence, and exile" indeed.

This terrible knowledge sustains a number of citizen poets. For Sam Abrams, the horrors in Bosnia make it necessary to scourge the polis by asking: "And how are we better than the good Germans, the so civilized French / who stood by, who averted their eyes?"

In her "Note from Memphis," Lucille Clifton knows that "history is chasing you, america / like a mean dog." Carolyn Kizer lists the victims, "Armenians, Jews / Gypsies, Russians, Vietnamese, / the Bosnians / the Somalians. . . ." And Elinor Nauen, quoting Freud quoting Heine, declares, "One must forgive one's enemies / but not before they have been hanged."

All these poets can be said to affirm their citizenship in this century, but there are degrees of awkwardness. Abrams, Clifton, Kizer, and Nauen do so with a straight face and thus make the strongest connection to Walt Whitman's nineteenth century. But for others, such certitudes become either hedged by absurdity or qualified by powerlessness. Eileen Myles ran for the presidency on a poetry-lesbian-feminist platform. Her mock-seriousness was not compromised by the knowledge that "100 years of the naked emperor / is more than my eyes can stand." Her presidential platform was "Not me." NOT ME. Now here is someone who understands herself: Elect the Not-I, as Fichte said. Not me, said the little red hen.

The clearest, and for that matter, least utopian goodbyes came from the grand elders who have lived in, seen, and questioned this century, having seen, as well, the shipwreck of presumptions big and small. The century belongs to them by virtue of their having survived it.

Speaking of his "impending demise," James Broughton, born in 1914, notes: "Some kind of cold comfort to know that / one will be lying about the ruins / with Ozymandias Mussolini / and all the other residue of the millennium." Robert Creeley asks only, sensibly: "But couldn't it all have been / a little nicer / as my mother'd say." And from Carl Rakosi, the great Objectivist, now in his eighties: "The state of the world . . . flaky."

Anselm Hollo, born in Finland, was a child during the Second World

War. Looking back, he sees that "whatever it ever was / fights among *capos*." The century's history was but a gang fight, a clash of mafiosi egos. Who the *capos* were and what they stood for is a mystery that everyone would like to solve. What is certain is that all the *capos*, from Stalin to Hitler, stood on pyramids of the skulls of other *capos*.

WHO DID IT? is a question these poets ask often. The "who" and "it" change, but the belief that there was a crime and that someone or something did it to us is unchanging. The *capos*, or those *capo* forces that Marxists and Neomarxists tagged and tag, are the object of many a poetic volley.

Racism gets it in John Yau's aesthetic, moral, environmental, ironic, trivial, and, ultimately, political question: "Will this spill finally bleach me?"

On the same subject, Jonathan Williams delivers a moralist's blast at the enfeebling of the American mind, from "lorena to tonya." There is much to gloss on here since I am an observer of popular culture, and I even know all the jokes. When I visited Milwaukee, a journalist took me to the site of Jeffrey Dahmer's house, now a vacant lot with a big sign that said AWAITING TOTS DAYCARE. An old man with a whip in his belt and a spatula in his hand was walking his fluffy poodle by the fence, and when he saw us, he said: "I didn't know him. Lived here 18 years. Maybe I saw him once or twice. First read about it in the paper." The journalist said, "You know what I think about Jeffrey Dahmer?" "What?" I said. " He was just like us—he wanted to eat his lovers and keep them forever. Like the eucharist." "Yeah, but we only do that *metaphorically*," I said. "Maybe." She didn't see much difference.

So you can add to the enfeebling of the American mind, the TV-induced inability to distinguish between literality and figurativeness. Eventually, every mother who says to her baby, "I will eat you all up," will do just that. That's the dystopian solution to the problem of hunger.

Terence Winch curses Carl Sagan in his poem, and with him, the antiseptic utopia of space salesmen. Like most real poets, Winch doesn't see space as the "ultimate frontier," but just an extension of the military-industrial complex to a place somewhere over our heads. A few years ago, before the *Challenger* blew up, there was some plan to put a poet in space.

One of the greatest gifts American technology has made to the living of our century is amnesia. But even amnesia comes in for a whacking, by Paul Auster, who regrets losing the details of his life through an American riddled brain. And Anne Waldman finds that she "forgot / I forgot something / amnesia of holocaust / amnesia for war & war & more war . . ." She has forgotten precisely that which is unforgettable. What we would like to forget, if only it were possible.

None of these culprits, to be sure, stand shelled for long. The more obvious sins of America are not so much excoriated as noted in their complex interplay with the poets themselves. It is Allen Ginsberg who most completely identified himself with his time and place. In his poem he accuses America of poisoning the world's air and water, but it is his own body that is America. "Fire Air Water tainted," he laments, followed by "poor circulation, smoke more cigarettes." Four decades have passed since the poet's curse, "America, go fuck yourself with your atom bomb!" In that time, Ginsberg and America merged. He, no less than the rest of us, stood no longer outside because the outside, like clean air and water, had vanished, another fin-de-siècle casualty.

One can hear a harsh urgency now in the work of those whose bodies have become the battlefield of a new American politics. Here, in the arena circumscribed by the body, even Judeo-Christianity gets a new job. "The Voice kept tugging at my ear," declares Jack Anderson in the persona of Noah, ". . . nagging and ordering me / to tell the people of the city, 'Because of your wickedness / this place will be destroyed.'" The place HAS been destroyed in the ravaged bodies of Michael Andre's friends: "the tragedy of the homosexual today—all I can do for / such friends is make this hello to the magnetic / pole of death that draws us like the years. / I make few prayers while this cold Pole is pope."

William Burroughs takes on Christianity in the flesh: "what about the Inquisition, that stinks of burning flesh, torture, excrement—its stultifying presence imposed by brutal force." The meek, for whom Christ apparently died, are all but forgotten. For Charles Bukowski, it's not worth living in a future where "hospitals are so expensive it's cheaper to die."

Bukowski is one of the few poets—Tom Dent was another—to speak on behalf of the downtrodden in a manner not checked by self-consciousness. From the 1930s to midcentury, such paucity of proletarian sympathy would have been shocking. Even more shocking to those distant ages of humanism would have been the radical doubts some poets have about the nature of humanity itself. Bruce Andrews produced an alphabetical list of words defined randomly by vaguely familiar found phrases. Rae Armantrout's faith is retained only by a question mark: "No one home / in the 'Virtual Village'? / Between the quote marks / nothing but disparagement."

Jack Marshall noted, with remarkable understatement: "Earth's not cherry anymore." A shattering malaise has entered the world and left its signature in fractured language, a medium no longer transparent, and badly suited for carrying understanding. All that remains are the shards of what we thought or had been made to think, shards that are vastly outnumbered by the things we make and buy. What did we think? What were we made to think? Whatever it was, it is late. "Ditto the caveat, ibid the scam," writes Bill Berkson. Some epitaph!

The elegiac calibrates even the densest texts, the most telegraphic notations. For some, here Charles Bernstein, the multiplication of products induces regret at having done anything at all: "The goats pass / from view, the boys / skip stones from / melancholy hydroplanes. / I should have wasted my life."

Without irony such sentiments would be tragic. But not necessarily. The world of bright, shiny, American-made objects has its fans. For David Trinidad, an Angeleno, the American century is the movies. He loves them, they are as complete a language as personal psychology.

Joe Cardarelli in "Against 21st Century," disdains the coming age of antiseptic living. He has loved his time and the abusive pleasures of his world. There are also ways of relishing the mess, as Pat Nolan suggests: "acquire a taste for the bitterseweet / it soothes that sinking feeling."

Jim Gustafson celebrates the joys of "not getting caught."

Still, an American *De Natura Rerum* is missing from this book, which is a mystery. In saying goodbye to their century, our poets were careful to note as Janine Pommy Vega does, "Noise, blood, suffering" but kept their distance from even those objects that DO appear occasionally in their poems.

Are there any hopeful goodbyes? Well, some of the women think so. They are able to see the future as something they will give birth to, something to nurture.

Janine Canan says: "Oh Century, my laborious Century! / Drop by Drop the blood-streaked columns thicken / and our ancient fire glows still." Bernadette Mayer prays for better men and women to inhabit the planet: "so therefore war father, mother, let me be & leave me / I know how to propagate the race for slightly peace that is / to only give birth to women: or to sweet loving boys who have in their builds / no desire to make us war or crazier."

Sex receives its homage but not as lyrically as was once the norm. Summer Brenner reports some "naked doric gals on Emerald Hill" who have no regret for having whooped it up.

Make no mistake: the sacred that enters the world of these poems has gotten here the hard way. It has made its way through beliefs and discarded beliefs. It has survived loves and Love. It has stared Death in the face. It has burrowed through the postmodern fragments of poetry and through the shopping malls. It has outlived the death of the twentieth century, a harsh father. It has asked, who will pay the century's "karmic debt"?

Alice Notley in her poem "DÉSAMÈRE," journeys through the desert, confronts evils and Evil, and finds, in the end, a commonality that transcends everything: "Brother, says Amère: 'Why are you and I / Like this . . . soldier, widow, / Why aren't we cars?'" This is the reply, in the voice of the poet Robert Desnos, "Because you grieve like animals . . . / Behaving as your species would / If it hadn't turned into cars / You're still the animals."

Here it is, all the tragicomic grotesquery of the spent century. It's not a fond farewell. No one seems to have liked the deceased. And yet everyone suspects that the convention of the artificially designated "twentieth century" held something profoundly significant. While it is true, says Jack Anderson, that "there is never an end . . . / of treachery / lies / stupidity, arrogance / brute force, and lost causes," there is also, as Arthur Sze puts it, the "moment when a child asks / when will it be tomorrow?"

Elaine Equi gives us the possibility that "you can . . . sleep now, gentle / reader, and dream of comets trailing blood and / planets exploding. When you wake, it will be spring." That would be nice. It would be nice, that is, if like the old movies, this narrative had a happy ending. It might have been possible if it had had a happy beginning, but, as Eileen Myles says, "the first thing we learned / was that the world would end / in our time." I was born in 1946, the year that the beginning and the end were one at Hiroshima. My co-editor, Laura Rosenthal, was born in 1958, at the beginning of rock 'n' roll. "That's the human song," says Alice Notley, "from the past to nowhere."

A Russian Poet at the Seashore

St. Petersburg, Florida, is what happens when you take out a box of pastels and paint in the sky, the houses, the bushes, and the people. Gold turned into pink then lavender then velvety blue over the Gulf of Mexico while evening-gowned, golf-course-tanned folks sailed past me, barely spilling a drop of their martinis or upsetting the cherry in the blue glasses. It was Sunday, November 5, 1995, and this was a literary soiree. I was holding on to my end of a toothpicked green olive, looking at the sunset, when someone whispered breathlessly in my ear that Yitzhak Rabin had been assassinated.

Did anybody else know? I whirled around but there wasn't a ripple in the crowd. I appointed myself bad-news bearer and went around informing the literati and the local oligarchy. It was a strange thing, like swimming through cotton wadding in a nightmare. Some knew, some didn't, but few did more than shake their heads, annoyed at the interruption. I didn't upset anyone very much until I told the Russian poet Yevgeny Yevtushenko, who made a huge, hurt noise and demanded to be led to a television set to watch the breaking news.

He and I and a friend of his plunked down in front of the mega-TV and began flipping channels looking for the expected coverage. But, man oh, man, it was only football games and quiz shows and old movies. What was going on? Had we hit a time warp? Every time we found another football game or quiz show or old movie, Yevtushenko exclaimed in frustration: "This is fascism!" And by that, he meant the extraordinary blitheness of TV at such a historic moment. Not to speak of the pastel crowd numbed by the surf and cocktails outside. Finally, we got to CNN and they were, of course, talking about it, but still they were running the sports scores at the bottom of the screen.

The Russian poet shook his head in disbelief. He had once been the first, in the now nearly forgotten days of communism, to brand the specter of Russian anti-Semitism in his famous poem "Babii Yar." Now, here he sat, under the Don-Cesare-pink sky of Florida, in the middle of a cocktail party, alone or nearly alone, with the big bad world. He suffered the news of Rabin's murder with an intensity that made his blue eyes deeper than the pastels around us.

"I must write about this!" he exclaimed, and I think that he meant everything: the passing of a peacemaker he admired, the indifference or seeming indifference of those around him, the unperturbed inanity of television. He was far from Russia, Yevtushenko, and even farther from the Soviet Union where he had once been as famous a man as the dead prime minister.

San Francisco's Poet Laureate

S an Francisco held a unique and noble event that ought to be emulated by cities around the country: the coronation of a poet laureate. The ceremony took place at the new and controversial San Francisco Library, which is reputed to have more computers than books. Mayor Willie Brown made the presentation with panache and patience. A mentally ill audience member screamed something about prisoners in Eritrea and a conspiracy against her dogs. But best of all, the laureate himself, poet Lawrence Ferlinghetti, delivered a blistering critique of his beloved city and bit eagerly the hand that anointed him.

San Francisco, Ferlinghetti told the crowd, is losing its soul to cars, a state he called Autogeddon. Gentrification, tacky money, and lack of respect for diversity and tradition are eating the city's soul. He attacked the navy's Blue Angels, which regularly shatter the peace. "The poetic life requires Peace, not War," the poet proclaimed, "The poetic life of the City, our subjective life, the subjective life of the individual is constantly under attack by all the forces of materialist civilization, by all the forces of our military industrial perplex, and we don't need these warplanes designed to kill and ludicrously misnamed the Blue Angels."

The poet laureate made a series of concrete proposals to restore the soul of San Francisco, including giving pedestrians and bicyclists priority over automobiles, making the city a low-power alternative for radio and TV, with tax breaks for broadcasters, and uncovering the city's creeks and rivers again to open riparian corridors to the bay. Then he urged everybody listening to vote YES on a proposition that would remove the Central Freeway from the skyline. He also called for the city to declare North Beach—where Ferlinghetti's unique bookstore, City Lights, is located—a "historic district like the French Quarter in New Orleans." I think that the poet was under the impression that the French Quarter was a car-free poetic zone, but I disabused him of that notion later when I told him the truth: The French Quarter has more cars than Formosan termites.

This marvelous display of conviction, poetry, and clarity was fresh water to an audience saturated, here as elsewhere, by the mind-boggling clichés of political scandal and the nauseating praise of business and money that waft from the open sewers of the media and politicians' mouths. The return of the citizen-poet is a necessity these days, if only to remind everyone that it is possible to speak forcefully and clearly about things that matter to a community. Cities without poets are cities without soul.

Poetic Terrorism

A group calling itself the Assault Poetry Unit dropped off an assortment of suspicious packages at various offices around New Orleans, including that of the *Times-Picayune* newspaper, which evacuated its employees. The package turned out to be a watermelon with a four-page manifesto in it. The editor of the *Times-Picayune* was at the time deeply immersed in discussing the upcoming social season with the paper's gossip columnist. They were forced instead to huddle under a freeway overpass with the manifesto, while the NOPD bomb squad dismantled the watermelon. The manifesto called for painting over the huge Marlboro Man ad at Decatur Street and replacing it with a poem by Ishmael Reed; it called for all Louisiana government speeches to be written and read in iambic pentameter; and it demanded that New Orleans police officers memorize and recite poems at regular intervals. It was perhaps this, more than anything else, that caused the police to treat the incident as a crime. The manifesto declared that "the era of poetic passivity is over," an egregious statement in a city where passivity, poetic or no, is a sacred institution, especially in the summer. We are so passive here that we never even shoo the flies away from our po' boys; even the donkeys pulling the tourists quit flicking their tails this time of the year; even more amazingly, no mayoral candidacies are declared at all, leaving the incumbent to take an unencumbered siesta. The energetic manifesto demanded, among yet more things, that the mayor read "The Brown Menace or Poem on the Survival of Roaches" by Audre Lord in its entirety on the seven o'clock news. Now, if someone would dare to wake Hizzoner up, that might solve the problem of what to put on the news, which has been all about how hot it is outside. Still, crime or no crime, you have to hand it to the Assault Poetry Unit. They ambulate, they agitate, they say something. In New Orleans, like in the rest of America now, that's the height of social action.

Solution: *Enivrez-Vous:*
The Bars of New Orleans

or with Kerri McCaffety in the
Realm of Timelessness

On a timeless afternoon in late summer in the courtyard at the Napoleon House, a huge palmetto bug stared up at a famous poet from Colorado, and the man shrieked. As he drew his legs up on the chair, pointing to the small shining being down there, he asked, "What is THAT?"

"It's a small hearse," one of the six local bohemians said.

"It takes visible bites out of pears," nodded another.

"It's a beauty. We should enter him in the contest," mused the poorest one among us, who was cadging drinks and always looking for strange ways to make a buck. The contest he was referring to takes place every year: It's between Louisiana and Texas over the size of local roaches.

The light was suspended between day and night, the air was velvet-thick, there were beads of sweat on everyone's forehead, and the palmetto kept looking up, antennae quivering like a recording device. And, indeed, I might contend that many of our outsized bugs are recording the secret history of New Orleans to pass on through the generations. Somebody has to record this history because, God knows, the humans who frequent the soulful dives of this licentious city are too busy making up stories to also remember them.

The lack of memory is amply supplanted by the wealth of verbiage that flows like the Mississippi through barrooms, saloons, music joints, cafés, and holes-in-the-wall. Some of this unbound orality is a way for natives of the same generation to recall the past, which in New Orleans never goes away but is continuously reinvented by storytelling. In old restaurants like Galatoire's or Antoine's, where the solemn food imparts an aristocratic aura to the drinking, the gentry counts its cousins and polishes its roots like the brass doorknobs on their uptown mansions. The waiters belong to families, and they cajole, correct, and dispense their own additions even as they glide in and out of the kitchen.

One lost patron who had not set foot in Galatoire's for fifteen years recognized her waiter of yore, who remembered not only her drink and her favorite dish of soft-shell crab, but set also to remonstrate her for her absence. When my friend explained somewhat peremptorily that she had been in exile somewhere in California, the waiter said that he, too, had been absent for five of those fifteen years, five years during which he had raised a family in Florida, beaten back a heroin addiction, and then returned to the only place where he felt needed. These confessions took a good twenty minutes, but no one showed any impatience: The physical details of food and drink were only olives in the cocktail of intimacy that is the true purpose of such an establishment.

If one is concerned with time and efficiency, as they are understood in the harried labor camps of most American cities, one would do well to stay out of New Orleans bars, or New Orleans altogether. The watering holes of this city lay claim to different hours, and their interiors change with the hour. There are places for the afternoon and early evening, like the Napoleon House, where in the carefully maintained decay, locals can impress out-of-towners with the size of the roaches and the melancholy of a vivid and shadowy past. Napoleon could have lived here, if he hadn't died, but the implication is that he *does* live here, upstairs perhaps, and that he might descend the curved staircase at any moment to join the conversation.

A summer afternoon in New Orleans can stretch to infinity over a few beers. One can daydream in the shimmering cool, with or without companions, until it is either late in the day or late in the century. It is a fact of New Orleans history that vast conspiracies have been hatched in the afternoons in bars and cafés. Besides the glorious failed plot to rescue the emperor himself from exile, numerous dreams of conquest and plunder rose in detail from local cups of absinthe, whiskey-laced coffee, and dark beer. Jean Lafitte's

Blacksmith Shop was where the famous pirate did business in plundered goods, and hatched depredations. A local adventurer twice conquered Nicaragua and declared himself emperor. The first U.S. war on Cuba was conducted from here by a certain Narcisso Lopez. Lee Harvey Oswald hung out in the French Quarter, broke and without much to do. I have myself sat with men who, for no visible reason, were seized by megalomaniac plans and visions of grandeur. I believe that the distortion of time, the twisted layout of the old buildings, the presence of stairwells, the slave quarters in the back of buildings, the wrought-iron balconies, the shameless flowering of per- fumed vines, the stultifying heat, and the indolence of the natives are the causes of such impulses.

The establishments of the night are quite different. Jazz was born in them and they are full of sound. Their purpose is violent exhibitionism, voyeurism, and varieties of sexual congress. Café Brasil, which is the brainchild of a Brazilian named Adé, is like a tropical tree full of chattering birds. Once planted into the sidewalk of Frenchmen Street, this café-bar-dancehall magnetized the whole neighborhood, re-creating a creolism straight out of George Washington Cable, complete with Brazilian accents. On the oppo- site side of the street is the venerable Snug Harbor, where music is the fore- ground but Carnival the perpetual background.

One would do well, as I have done many times, to investigate a single place over time, at different times of the day. Molly's on the Market, for in- stance, is home in the early afternoon to a lively Window Gang consisting of a varying crew of journalists, men-about-town, women-about-town, writ- ers of fiction and poetry, mysterious characters either larger or brighter than life, led on by Jim Monaghan, proprietaire extraordinaire, Irish wit and provocateur. Monaghan's extravagant personality imbues the day, but the night belongs to the tribes of the tattooed and pierced young. At night, a sloshed picture gallery displays itself with sensual impertinence. The beauty of Molly's is that it is not, whether in the daytime or at night, the exclusive preserve of an age or income group. Unlike the sterile night scenes of pre- tentious San Francisco or New York, Molly's (and most other New Orleans bars) welcomes all ages, all colors, and all sexual persuasions, provided that they are willing to surrender to the atmosphere.

A reporter from *The Wall Street Journal* sought me out in an effort to ex- plain a grim statistic that maintained New Orleanians live, on the average, ten years less than most Americans. We repaired to one of my favorite watering holes where we discussed this, and many other things besides, at great length. Around 3 A.M. an exquisitely beautiful young woman wrapped in a sarong that allowed for two multicolored reptiles to be seen entwined on her back, climbed on the bar and unwrapped herself, displaying to everyone the rest of the Laocoönian scene, in which the snakes, beginning at her coccyx, circled flowering vines to descend from her shoulders to her perineum. It was a magical moment, like a door opening suddenly to another world. The inkster of *The Wall Street Journal* was transfixed like a deer in the headlights of the moment, understanding in a flash that the grim statistic he was trying to explain was a figment of time, whereas what unfolded before him belonged to timelessness. This insight, thoroughly forgotten, illuminated yet some of his article, which said, "Yes, it's true, but . . ."

Yes, it's true that, statistically, we live less than people who go to bed at a plain hour in the joyless working hells of virtuous towns, but we live experientially twice as long. Having stayed up in the bars and saloons of New Orleans for a few years now, I can attest to their life-enhancing qualities. Some of them are veritable time machines. I know a three-hundred-year-old man who occupies the stool at the far end of the Saturn Bar. His longevity is the result of having no idea what time it is. He hasn't seen a newspaper in two hundred years. He is plotting to rescue Napoleon from exile, boredom, and history.

Part Two

In Defense of

Innocence

Bad Childhoods

I just read, for the first time, Mary McCarthy's *Memories of a Catholic Girl-hood*. It's a great book, the revenge of a brilliant writer on those who made her childhood hell. McCarthy was an orphan. She spent the early years of her life in the custody of a horrid pair of relatives and in the chilling shadow of rich grandparents who had everything but human warmth to give.

Some of these people's rules and regulations about children and life were still popular when I was growing up. In many of my friends' houses there were rooms where we children were forbidden to enter. Whippings were quite common, and the father with the belt was universally feared. Luckily, I didn't have one, and my stepfather's occasional efforts had little effect. I remember also dinners where the paterfamilias got to eat all kinds of delicacies while the children ate some thin borscht. Some kids couldn't play with their own toys so they wouldn't "wear them out."

Happily, these kinds of cruelties have gone out of fashion for the most part. Childhoods are doubtlessly still difficult, but not horrid. My own kids were overindulged in almost everything. My oldest, Lucian, who's now an engineer, used to create awful scenes if he was interrupted from gluing his billion-piece models by something as trivial as dinner. He would be dragged kicking and screaming from his glue vapors in order to be given chemical-free nutrition. My other son, Tristan, benefited from such liberty that he needed only to make a phone call to spend the week drumming in the woods. Parents have relaxed considerably since McCarthy's days, and the coming generations should be grateful. Surely there will always be childhood sorrow because children's pain is magnified hundredfold by their lack of reference, but it won't be of the intensity that caused Mary McCarthy to cry her spendid cri de coeur.

In light of this, what is one to make of all the adults who now claim they were raped by their parents who cooked and ate their playmates in satanic ceremonies? Are these just the paranoid delusions of unhappy children or are the monster parents of yore reincarnated even more monstrously because so many parents now are kinder and more indulgent? These are all questions to be raised in a course on unhappy childhood memoirs, which I will teach sometime. I plan to reread Somerset Maugham's *Of Human Bondage,* too.

Innocence Lost Under Capitalism!

Dilema is a Romanian cultural journal that calls itself a "transition weekly." It has chronicled the changes from state socialism to nouveau capitalism in all its aspects. One of the most touching discoveries it has made is that capitalism has been stealing the innocence of Romanian children. Professor Dorel Zaica from Bucharest had been asking children questions since the 1970s, things like: "What is fog?" "What is peace?" "What are fingernails for?," and "Why do cat's eyes light up at night?" In the 1970s, during the Ceauşescu dictatorship, children said things like, "Fog is a lit-up darkness," and "Grass is a creature that wants to beautify our country," and "Peace is a silence made by a man with a trumpet." The professor continued asking his questions after the collapse of the dictatorship and noticed that by 1996, the kids were becoming very well informed and quite reasonable. If the kids of 1970 said that the picture on a stamp was a drawing of the street where the letter was supposed to go, the kids of 1996 said things like: "A stamp is an identification card for a letter." The kids of 1970 believed that "old people's hair got white because their hearts were getting white," but in 1996, they said that "Hair gets white in old age, instead of blue or purple, so we won't look ridiculous on the street like some old women." Mr. Cesar-Paul Badescu, the editor of this children's column, notes that today children have "lost their spontaneity and childish irrationality." They are well-informed by television, they are witty, intelligent, have ecological attitudes even—in other words, "they are just like adults."

I grew up in the information-void of the precapitalist era in Romania, and I remember the magical power of knowing very few facts and using my imagination to make up the world. In fact, I still avoid facts like the plague in the hope that I can stay sufficiently childish to amuse myself and others. Alas, the juggernaut of ponderous truths, minute observations, news, and vérité-floods keep rolling in and evicting whatever stubborn facility for invention we once had.

One can't feel really sorry for the newly plugged-in Romanian children, but how can one not miss an assertion like, "Time is something you don't know if it's coming or passing."

But it's passing, passing. That's the truth.

The Unabomber in School

One of the cruelest assignments I ever gave my students was to read the entire Unabomber Manifesto from *The Washington Post*. In addition, they were to write an essay on it. It is a testimony to their toughness that they got through the whole text without dropping the class. To tell you the truth, and this confession will get me in big trouble, I couldn't get past the middle of it; my eyes glazed over, the pencil fell from my hand, and I fell into an agitated sleep wherein I stood before my class, which had grown to millions of people somehow, and they were all shouting at me: You Are Trying To Bore Us to Death! Be that as it may, their observations were right on target: one person could actually *hear* a Midwestern accent in the perfectly bland sentences. Another wrote a little play in which she had him living in a remote cabin in the mountains. Between us we sleuthed him up pretty good but then the class decided that one of us, a kid who didn't speak much, was really the Unabomber. And, by God, when he pulled the hood of his jersey over his head, he WAS it. One student, a young writer who works at one of New Orleans's finest restaurants, told us that she had asked a shy Cuban dishwasher who had a crush on her to download the manifesto from the Internet. It was as if she'd consented to marry him. The shy dishwasher turned out to be a computer freak who lived in a basement full of electronics and had an active fantasy life that my student hoped she wasn't too big a part of. In any case, he brought her the manifesto plus a foot-high stack of related documents: comments on the manifesto, bomb recipes, poetry. She staggered under the load but one look at his beaming face and she knew it: Xavier, the shy Cuban dishwasher, was the Unabomber! Now that the actual item seems to be in custody, we, seekers after knowledge, are bereft. On the one hand, we are relieved to never have to wade through such tedious prose; on the other, we miss the excitement of suspecting each other of being terrorists. Ah, well.

The Art of Escape

In 1959, when I was thirteen years old, I found the Ursuline nuns' coin collection on top of a cabinet in our school chemistry lab. The box was a small wooden casket with a sliding top filled with Greek and Roman gold and silver coins minted between 27 B.C. and A.D. 200

Our school was a former Ursuline teaching convent, renamed the Red Star Elementary School Number 2. It was connected to a closed Catholic church built in the year 1723, a Baroque fortress in whose mossy walls you could still make out cannonballs left behind by a forgotten Turkish siege. Tunnels led from the school to the church and from the church to the outside of the city walls. Fifteen generations of nuns were buried in the walls of these tunnels, which had also been used for escape into the surrounding mountains. The Turks, who occupied the city several times, were particularly fond of nuns.

I am reminded of the Getty Museum in Los Angeles, which—not three hundred years old—does have the potential yet for living through a Turkish siege. And moss-covered cannonballs wouldn't look too bad embedded in all the Italian walls. In fact, Disney could stage a Turkish siege—for practice. Give any place three hundred years and it will experience a Turkish siege, sooner or later.

In any case, *our* fortress had undergone little or no change from the time the nuns lived there. Their classrooms were our classrooms, and their cells housed teachers' offices. We met in their prayer halls for our young communist indoctrination and self-criticism sessions. The chemistry lab had also been theirs. The retorts, burners, and chemical containers dated from the end of the last century. There were also some dusty glass cases behind which copper alembics and medieval jars lay neglected. In the floor-to-ceiling wooden cabinets there were rare birds' feathers, large and small eggs, a narwal horn, teeth from different animals, small skulls, shells, fish skeletons, bones of every shape and size, snake skins, pressed plant books, and samples of petrified and dried wood.

The nuns' laboratory was a wondrous kunstcamera whose chiaroscuro mystery served two purposes: It was a lesson in the magic of the bounty of forms in the natural world, and it was the perfect place to test the chemistry of sexual attraction when you could bend over a test tube with your crush of the moment.

There wasn't much chemistry being taught in the lab because for most of my four years there we didn't have a chemistry teacher. What we had was an hour each week when we could either study in the dusty and scary old lab or go to the school garden and sit with our books under the withered apple trees. Most kids went to the garden and pretended to read, but I preferred the old lab, especially if I could lure the studious and philosophically inclined Dulcea there, a serious girl with black eyes and chestnut hair who did, eventually, become a famous doctor.

But the day I found the nuns' coin collection I was alone.

I took out three gold Roman denarii bearing the heads of Octavian, Tiberius, and Claudius, and put them in my pocket. Every week I added three more gold coins to my collection and put the box back on top of the shelf. Eventually there were no more gold coins and I had forty pieces at home, hidden behind my small bookshelf containing, among other things, the complete works of Mark Twain translated into Romanian, all the Jules Verne novels I could find, and *Three Men in a Boat* by Jerome K. Jerome, the funniest book ever written.

For almost a year, when I was alone in the house I would take out my Roman coins, turn out all the lights, and feel them, living out fantasies I have now forgotten but that were adventurous and delicious and substituted for masturbation which I didn't discover until my fifteenth year—which doesn't yet bring me to the subject of this essay, but it gets us closer.

My stepfather's mother, a shrewd peasant woman who loved money above all else, came to live with us for a month when I turned fourteen. In one of those moments when she had my whole attention I told her that I was the owner of a great treasure. My parents were somewhat inured to my stories, and they had dismissed my statements to that effect with condescending ennui over the past year. But the old woman believed me. So I showed her. Forty heads of Roman emperors on rounded lumps of gold. Together we conceived a plan to find out just how much my treasure was worth. In Stalinist Romania in the 1950s owning gold was forbidden to individuals and there were severe punishments involved. A perennial charge against Jews was their ownership of illegal gold. An entire family from next door had been dragged out of their beds in the middle of the night and arrested after Securitate officers dug up our courtyard. We never saw them again.

So there were risks. Our plan involved my taking a single coin to the Bruckenthal Museum and asking to see an archaeologist. I would then tell him that I'd found it near Ocna Sibiului, a village five miles from the city, where there were Roman digs.

The archaeologist smoked while he studied the coin. I had chosen one at random. "This is very exciting," he said after a very long time, "Tiberius. No Tiberius denar was ever found in Romania."

"That's right," I said, beaming with pride. "This is the first time."

The archaeologist gave me a choice. I could show him the exact location of my find and then have my name inscribed in the annual bulletin of the Bruckenthal Museum, which was the greatest honor conceivable, or I could sell him the coin for five Romanian lei.

I went home to ponder my choice and to consult with my step-grandmother.

"It would be a great honor indeed," the old woman said, "to have your name inscribed in the annual bulletin of the Bruckenthal Museum."

"Yes," I countered, "but five leis will buy two Jules Verne novels I don't have."

"Or a pair of pants," she said.

"Or two eclairs with whipped cream at the Flora." I was warming up to the game. I then thought of all my delicious fantasies of being a Roman and buying a sailboat—a trireme—and wowing naked natives with my wealth. I said, "But think how much more this gold coin must have been worth in Roman times."

The fact that the gold coin was worth more in the past seemed logical to me. The coin was after all *old*, and we were steeped in the knowledge that the past was a dank and filthy place of exploitation and misery while the future, particularly the communist future, was shiny, glorious, and golden. "Golden" was the adjective to describe the future under all circumstances. So what we had here was the natural progression of things from a once-powerful but devalued past to a shiny but yet unrealized future. The past had actually decayed and become worthless while the future was being prepared. That something once worth a sailboat was now worth only a pair of pants seemed natural to me.

The shrewd old woman did nothing to discourage this belief.

I went back to the archaeologist. "I have thought about this long and hard, and while I would very much like the honor of having my name inscribed in the annual bulletin of the Bruckenthal Museum, I don't think that I can remember exactly where I found this coin. So I'll take the five leis."

"Five leis?" the archaeologist exclaimed indignantly, "Whoever gave you the idea that you'd get five leis for something you don't remember finding?"

"I remember finding it," I said. "I just don't remember where."

"The point is that you have something here that is wrapped in mystery. Two leis. That's it."

Now two leis didn't even buy *one* eclair. Or even one Jules Verne.

"In that case," I said, "I think that I'll have to think about it some more."

"On the other hand," mused the archaeologist, "if you had two, or, let's say, three of these, I could offer you ten leis for the three of them."

I went back to consult with the shrewd old woman and we came to the following conclusion. I would take three coins to the archeologist and get ten leis. She would take the rest of my coins with her to the village where she lived and she would bury them in a secret place known only to herself and to me. This seemed very logical to me so I took the three coins to the archaeologist, got ten leis, bought two Jules Verne novels, and the old woman took the money with her back to her village and buried them in a secret place whose exact location she never disclosed to me—and now she's been dead for lo, these past thirty years.

I spent a great deal of time in the Bruckenthal Museum. Even before I'd sold my coins to the archaeologist, I spent all my spare time in the mysterious twilight coolness of the Bruckenthal painting galleries. I was a lonely kid, living an intense fantasy life, and besides reading, the only thing I liked to do was look at the Flemish paintings in the Bruckenthal. These Flemish paintings, by Vermeer, van Eyck, and Rembrandt, had come to the Bruckenthal as gifts to Baron von Bruckenthal, governor of Transylvania, from the Austrian empress Maria Theresa, who was rumored to have been his lover. Whether that was true or not, Maria Theresa, the most prudish ruler of that bureaucratic empire, liked to drop off a canvas from the Vienna Gallery in the baron's palace whenever she came to visit. Which was quite often, judging by the great number of works in the museum. Baron von Bruckenthal was famous for his ingenuity, and particularly for having invented the rack-wheel, a torture device he had created specifically to provide a very painful death for the leader of a peasant rebellion named Horia. The rack-wheel that crushed Horia to death with its metal spikes had a place of honor in the Bruckenthal Museum, along with some other devices, such as an Iron Maiden and a Procrustean bed. This too was one of my favorite rooms, providing my adolescent sexuality with some powerful metaphors for the so-called torments of love, which I suffered in abundance nearly every day.

I divided my time equally between the still lifes of rich Dutch burghers and their portraits, and the baron's ancient torture devices, living inside a deep and detailed succession of imaginary worlds. I am convinced that a structural analysis of my mind would reveal a glistening fish on a platter next to a large onion below a hanging duck, while off-stage a bosomy Flemish servant is wiping her forehead with a corner of her dress revealing a milky white thigh and no underwear. Stretched on a torture rack behind her is my very own pale, skinny body with the off-stage voice of Aurelia saying, "Not yet. Not yet."

Aurelia, my girlfriend, said that a lot.

And I still hadn't discovered masturbation.

That discovery occurred almost a year after I had bedded not Aurelia, but Marinella, the school trollop, in a hayloft above a goatshed on the grounds of the local mental hospital. Suffice it to say that a year after that experience I found myself atop our living-room Biedermeier armoire next to a chipped marble statuette of Napoleon with his hand in his vest, an object my mother had carried, along with a few other possessions, across the border into Romania on the night that Hitler ceded Northern Transylvania to Hungary. I owe my existence to this border crossing; the fact that Napoleon crossed with my mother should have imbued him with significance for me, but I'm quite sure that this was not on my mind when I discovered masturbation. As

I successfully concluded this startling new discovery, my mother walked in early from work, and the last drops of my adolescent effluvium nearly landed on her head as she opened the door.

She pretended not to see me there next to Napoleon, and the incident was all but forgotten. It would be an understatement to say that I lived in a dream for my first fifteen years, but it would be accurate to note that the dream I lived in was a dream of art, composed equally of imagination and history.

I will let you and myself off this embarrassing hook by recounting only one other historical intersection of art and nascent sexuality. At some point at the end of the fifties, the torture instruments at the Bruckenthal were replaced by a collection of artifacts purporting to glorify communism. The torture room became the room of the History of the Communist Party, and most of it was taken up by a huge bronze sculpture of a locomotive on top of which stood Lenin with his arm outstretched. This was *Lenin Arriving at the Finland Station* and it was big enough to hide behind and make out. Plus nobody ever went into the History of the Communist Party room, whereas the torture room had been quite popular. I must thus include Lenin on a locomotive among the significant objects of my first wave of sexuality.

The proper appreciation of art does not begin in college, not even in high school; it does not begin after the advent of sexuality; and it doesn't have anything to do with the opinions of experts, or rather, it can be the result of the opinion of *any* experts. The experts who organized the art-world of my childhood were only modest connoisseurs: a gigolo-baron, my mother with her prized statuette of Napoleon, a shrewd old woman who robbed me, an archaeologist who did the same, and a provincial communist party organization. Art assumes its significance in the psyche when it grows in the fertile soil of innocence and imagination, aided by history.

When I look at paintings, sculpture, photography, or any other kind of image now, I listen foremost for the echo of that time before time when things were generators of fantasy. When something strikes me, it is because traveling through time on some stretch of pigment or sheen of stone is a world I have now mostly forgotten.

> Traveler, oh, traveler, where headest thou?
> To the light of my birth, to my first how.

The Pleasures of Art

I met my painter wife, Alice, in 1965. We lived on New York's Lower East Side. She studied at the New York Studio School, an abstractionist enclave, while I worked at the 8th Street Bookstore, an avant-garde haunt of poets. At that time, poets and painters were great friends. The covers of books by Frank O'Hara, James Schuyler, Ted Berrigan, Ed Sanders, and scores of others were graced by the art works of Red Grooms, Alex Katz, Joe Brainard, George Schneeman, Donna Reed, and many others.

The mid-sixties were a playful time. Poets played with words, artists played with their materials, poets played with artists, and artists played with poets. What made these playful times significant was that this playfulness was serious business. The adult world was going to hell. Young men were dying in Vietnam, young protesters were teargassed on the streets, the Soviets pointed their nukes at us, we pointed our nukes at them, and, according to most thinkers, the world as we knew it was going to end in a heap of rubble in our time. Our response to this state of affairs was to question "the world as we knew it," and to see if there wasn't some way out of this grim agreement, by uncovering worlds as we didn't know them. The key to such uncovering was in play. The seriousness of doomsayers was challenged by a myriad of artistic alternatives. Art burst the confines of canvas, questioned patronage, privilege, and aesthetic definition. Museums were regarded with as much suspicion as police stations.

The revolutionary playfulness of art in the sixties was not new to art. It proceeded from the very beginning of the consciousness that saw fit to create artifacts that were separate from nature and that fixed the forms of an artist's perception into some kind of material. That consciousness is as old as art itself and is present in all art, including ritual and religious art. In ritual and religious art there is inscribed also a mnemonic of the ritual, but that is the art's most fragile characteristic and tends to disappear as soon as the ritual is no longer practiced.

Some of the most enduring conventions of art were challenged successfully in my own time by the spirit of play. Andy Warhol's paintings, collages, silkscreens, and films, for instance, challenged the separation of art from commerce, daily life, other arts, and drawingroom seriousness. Joe Brainard's extraordinary number of small collages, including some on matchbooks, questioned the value and pricing of art objects. Some of them sold as cheaply as ten leis, if I remember correctly. The high-minded purism of abstractionists was deflated by pop artists. Going back in the history of art one can make an easy argument, of course, for the succession of styles under the pressure of new aesthetic convictions. But this is not what I am talking about. The period I am describing aimed not just at overthrowing the aesthetic conventions of the older generation, but art itself, including the products of the artists themselves. The surrealists had discussed this issue at length and they had resolved, at least theoretically, that the process of the imagination was more important than its products. The irony of the present, which is that the products are now valued as products with little or no regard for the process, is only one of the many ironies that were self-evident to us in the sixties but are no longer either self-evident or important enough to uncover.

Which brings me to the true subject of this essay, which is irony. Just kidding. But to mention only one night in a long series of nights in the mid-sixties—a time that consisted mostly of long nights—I went to visit the great American poet Ted Berrigan at 3 A.M., his favorite hour, and I found him in the process of rearranging the pictures on his walls.

"You're here just in time," he said, "to help me rearrange the pictures on my walls." Besides being one of Ted's favorite late-night activities, the rearranging of his artworks was one of the great Socratic occasions that we younger poets drew spiritual sustenance from. Along with the rearranging of pictures came great disquisitions on art, the artists who had made them, and the general philosophy of art as it applied to our own attempts to making it. Ted had a couple of Andy Warhols, three Alex Katzes, a Fairfield Porter, many works by George Schneeman and Joe Brainard, collages and photographs by Rudy Burckhardt, paintings by Donna Reed. All these were gifts and he prized them highly. Rearranging them was a way to see them anew, to discover previously unknown relationships between them, and to view them metaphorically and literally as descriptions of our minds at this particular time. The reason I can never remember exactly what artworks Ted owned is because in his disquisitions he rarely mentioned the names of the artists or the artworks we were rearranging. There was obviously no need of it since we were looking at the works as we were rearranging them. Later, however, both memory and tapes fail to yield the specifics, while tending to highlight the brilliant, aphoristic quality of Ted's mind, which proposed such things as: "All portraits would look better if they had a balloon over their heads that said, 'Hi, Folks!'"

In addition to writing poetry, most of us poets also made collages, drawings, paintings, little sculptures, and lots of other, undefinable objets. The reason for this, I am not ashamed to say, was that we smoked a lot of marijuana, which focused our attention on the details of our world like nothing else could. Marijuana made us playful and took us back to our childhoods. Later, it did other things, like make us paranoid, but this is not the subject of this essay. Big History may not look indulgently on our efforts, but the history of art may not dismiss them entirely, if for no other reason than that they were unique objects with limited distribution and we all know how rarity makes its own value. We didn't care much about history—at least I didn't—while being acutely conscious of the deployment of history above, below, and in us. What our activities aimed for was the sabotage of history, its overthrow, which—as some philosophers now tell us—has come about through overproduction. I can argue with this, but this is not the subject, etc.

What I do know, from having lived through this playful and unusually grave period of the twentieth century, is that it was possible, for a brief moment, to reconnect with the imagination of childhood and have almost as much pleasure as a lonely Transylvanian child in a dark museum full of torture instruments. I say "almost as much" because the pleasures of art-making in the sixties were interwoven with an active sexuality that could never be quite as free as pre-sexuality.

Which brings me back to my wife, the painter.

Her work was fresh, forceful, colorful, and simple. At first she painted big and abstract, the way they taught her at the Studio School, but you could always tell that flowers and people were trying to push through the thick pigment—texture was Studio School gospel—and assert themselves. Colors and light and real shapes were natural to her, so as soon as she left school and we went to the West Coast, she started painting flowers, plants, clouds, children, and the Russian River in different lights. Northern California was particularly suited for watercolors. She also drew witty and somewhat skeptical cartoons, the skepticism being a survival ingredient in a milieu of mystically inclined counterculturists and naturists who, not content with being young, rebellious, and naked, also spouted many happy clichés. Alice's artworks surrounded me in California, and it is almost impossible to think of those days without seeing her bright, energetic, happy colors.

Between 1970 and 1975 the light in California had a quality that I haven't seen after that, a quality some have called "psychedelic," and which, I have no doubt, proceeded from a certain induced perception of the world but was there nonetheless. This quality was in addition to the fifteen obvious qualities of light that are still there. This kind of light left the state around 1977 and it hasn't been back since, making Alice's paintings of the time documentary as well as unique.

After 1977, American life became museumified for me, though I am willing to argue that it became so for America as well. A sociopsychological study of a certain loss of innocence might be in order—but this, again, is not my subject. Museums, on the other hand and since we are in one, are part of my subject. Museums, and I might as well speak plainly here, are the enemies of art. Libraries, let me clarify, are not the enemies of books, but museums are the enemies of art.

The ambiguity of the relationship between artists and the institutions or people who patronize them is nothing new. One of the best expressions of this ambiguity may be found in Alice Neel's series of paintings entitled *Men in Suits*. Alice Neel's men in suits cover the range from art collectors to famous artists to notorious radicals to her own son, Richard, who became a banker. All these men, indifferent of their occupations, live within the straitjacket of a suit. The painter, while bemoaning the loss of freedom symbolized by these suits, does not, in any way, simplify the men within. She paints their complexity and also her dependence on them as an artist and a woman. The ambiguity of love for her subjects and contempt for the lives they've chosen recapitulates the ontogeny of the artist-state, artist-society, and artist-museum relationship. This ambiguity may be found in perfect form in La Fontaine's fable "The Ant and the Grasshopper," which he got from Aesop, so we know that even the Greeks felt it.

So what is my subject? Only this. A museum, a society, a state, or any institution in the business of art should try to re-create a state of pre-adolescence for its audience. The happy coincidence of an encounter be-tween a collection of torture implements and an overwrought imagination is one possibility. In a certain sense, no matter how many experts there are carefully tending to art history, the arbitrariness will manifest itself soon enough. In the last two decades, arbitrariness has, in fact, speeded up like almost anything else in contemporary life. Nothing looks more dated than certainly willful formal experiments of modernism that aimed, paradoxically, for timelessness. On the other hand, innocence and (pre) sexuality, as well as wisdom and sexuality, are rarely available to those who take themselves too seriously. Money tends to make people serious. Art does the opposite. If the twain shall ever meet—and sometimes they do—money should adopt the playfulness of art, and never, never, the other way around. When art adopts the seriousness of money, it becomes money. When money becomes as playful as art, it becomes art. And that, in my opinion, is the way to live.

Not So Fruit: Three Paintings
by Amy Weiskopf

ONE: *STILL LIFE WITH MOZZARELLA*

In a dramatic tableau worthy of the sixteenth-century still-life master Juan Sánchez Cotán, three tied-up mozzarella cheeses lord over five black olives, three onions facing three other onions, and a long-tailed garlic clove. The drama is really a farce, yet the tension is palpable. The cheeses are so ripe, their juice is overflowing. One of them has even cracked, so rife is it with power, age, and whiteness. The olives, like a fearful gang of thieves, are advancing on the cheeses with obscure intentions, intending either to rob them or beg them for favors. On a separate field of battle, the two onion threesomes are pursuing some kind of quarrel as deeply obscure as the shadow that lies between them. The onions are aroused, their tails and stalks are ruffled and standing. One gets the feeling that this is only a mock argument for the sake of entertaining the cheeses that protect them. Only the garlic looks (uncertainly) aware of the farcical nature of the relationships involved and, perhaps, of the illusory nature of all existence. This philosophical garlic is attempting to formulate a proper response to its devastating vision of tenuousness. One possibility is to escape from the tableau altogether, and to this end, the philosopher-garlic has already positioned itself (with the help of its creator) at the edge of the table whence a leap into nothingness is only a flip away. But the other possibility, expressively conveyed by its tail, is some kind of accommodation with the all-powerful cheeses whose attraction it cannot deny.

Salvador Dalí called garlic "the moon-flower of the Mediterranean," and explained that El Greco became a great painter only when he encountered the mystic spirit of Spain, just like an insipid snail, which is nothing before it encounters the mystical force of garlic. Amy Weiskopf, riding the centuries-old pictorial gastro-philosophy of the Mediterranean, gives garlic its time-honored philosophical role. *Still Life with Mozzarella* is a Garlic Farce, a time-honored form which, like the sonnet, never grows tired, because garlic is immortal.

The paradox of food in paintings is that it never rots, though the painter might push it to the very edge of ripeness. The aged mozzarellas have improved with time, though their decadent status raises interesting questions about power, freshness, and centrality. The aesthetics of the near-rotten cheeses and the pickled but penurious olives does battle with the juicy, young onions and the philosophical garlic. Looking over three hundred or so years of history, one can have little doubt of the outcome of this encounter. The onion, the postmodern vegetal par excellence, has won the metaphorical victory. The onion, consisting of layers, has no center. The soul, as embodied by garlic, has been relegated to the outside of the discussion, and the overripe cheeses have been assigned to the class enemy. But if one looks over three hundred years of culinary history, one finds that the garlic has triumphed, the onion has never been demoted (not even by shallots), and that mozzarella has remained confined to the Mediterranean (despite the success of its powdered simulacrum kin used in the New World over spaghetti).

Amy draws shameless attention to the numbers of her vegetables because you cannot be taken seriously in this world if you're not backed up by numbers. Every dabbler in the occult sciences from Paracelsus to John of Patmos to a marketing researcher knows the power of numbers. You can't sell without numbers, but for the purposes of persuasion any numbers will do. Are there five olives because the humble and the puny always draw together in such unstable quantities? Are there six onions divided in two groups because peasants are generically factional? Are there three mozzarella because big cheeses always rule by triumvirate? And is there only one garlic because philosophers are always lonely and irreducible? The numbers (any numbers) are a red flag to schizophrenics that the structural underpinnings of the universe are present and that they, like vegetables, are available for reflection.

89

TWO: *VANITAS WITH SKULL*

Painters, just like poets, have never tired of *vanitas*, because the persistent presence of Death has always put in question the material world. Just how thick or how transparent is matter? How do forms change under the pressure of mortality? If all is in vain, why not party? In the Middle Ages, Christianity produced an overabundance of symbolic reminders that Death and Judgment were at hand. Death was certainly at hand, but Judgment was another matter, reserved mainly for those who couldn't afford indulgences. The painters who undertook to depict the material luxuries that would surely pass as "a flower of the field," took great delight in their objects. The lesson, delivered usually by the skull, was just a rhetorical flourish. Quite often, the skull was itself a delightful and vain object. The well-accoutred study of a philosopher or even of a student would have been remiss without a skull. The skull authorized any debauches, whether intellectual or carnal, precisely because it was a reminder of the transitory nature of life. Drinking from a skull was de rigueur for bon vivants, and using skulls for candleholders was a cliché of student life that remains to this day.

The *vanitas* were debauches under the guise of morality, just like overly detailed descriptions of sins that aroused the worshippers to desires they sometimes undertook to satisfy right in church. The Protestant revolution was certainly aware of this Catholic excuse for pleasure, so *vanitas* were discouraged. Purged of sacred reminders, the *vanitas* became just still lives. Why anyone would undertake to paint *vanitas* now, as Amy Weiskopf has done, is an interesting question.

Obviously, she relishes the formal play of so many variously shaped objects, but that is a discussion for specialists. I am more intrigued by the stories this work suggests. There are several. The first is that the *vanitas* continue to say something about our time, despite the postmodern abolishment of simple dialectical opposition. The Reformation and the Counter-Reformation continue to battle for souls even now, long past the Enlightenment and well into the Information Age. The sly comment of this *Vanitas* is made by the position of the table, which makes it certain that everything on it, including the skull, is going to topple any minute. In fact, it's a miracle (of art) that the objects haven't yet toppled. This is *contra nat-*

uram, just like the persistence of Manichaean debate. The joke is that everything, not just the stuff on the table but also the *vanitas* genre itself, didn't long ago slide off the edge of the world. It is possible that when the first *vanitas* were painted, the world wasn't yet round.

The objects themselves are not particularly wicked to the contemporary viewer. The drinking goblets are collectible (besides, they are empty), the book is not from the Index Maleficorum, the plates and the bottle are clean. The skull is dust-free. There is a lemon on the table, looking very much at home except for the fact that it should have rolled off a long time ago. A lemon, a starfish, an olive, and some dice are balancing on a ledge *under* the table. The objects under the table do not look as if they had rolled off the table. On the contrary, they seem to want to roll off on their own. The dice, especially, are very eager to roll, but like everything else, they are subject to the amused control of the painter.

In this painting, as in many other of Weiskopf's works, the faux-solid shapes that are about to topple laugh gently at our certainties. They will never topple, but the threat gives us vertigo because, on the one hand, we would like to see them fall, and on the other we know that we can't do a thing about it. The painting is laughing at us but also at itself. The cups are so proud, the plate is so exhibitionistic, the lemon so rollicky. The objects are so serious, so grave, so well represented, that they are inevitably funny. They are businesslike and stolid like Dutch burghers with watches hanging over round bellies. You gotta love them, but they are going to fall. Not really. Let them eat paradox.

THREE: *MERLITONS AND SATSUMI*

Every Christmas in my black-and-white childhood we had the Miracle of Oranges. Direct from Haifa in the Promised Land, big, thick-skinned oranges appeared in the bare-shelf stores of Romania, and people queued up for miles to buy them. The four oranges—there was a limit of four—became the centerpiece of our table. No one would have dreamed of eating them before five days of contemplation had elapsed. At the end of those five days, at midnight on Christmas Eve, we peeled the bright round miracles and sucked in slice by slice the bright sun concentrated in them. These oranges cured fevers and set the year on its path.

The magic of my Haifa oranges clings to Amy Weiskopf's satsumi, in *Merlitons and Satsumi*, although her small, sweet Louisiana oranges follow a different agenda. They are actors in a sexual drama involving a complex and amused cabala. The merliton, or "alligator pear" of Louisiana, straddles the border between fruit and vegetable. It is a squash that looks like a pear or a large crab apple. Together, the satsumi and the merlitons proclaim the region, but just how do they do that? Individually, their specificity has already been invested with all the meanings they might hold. Satsumi can be popped in the mouth whole, peeled and sectioned, or put in the fruit salad. The merliton can be stuffed with crawfish or meat or cheese or another vegetable. Like any squash, it can be boiled, given a supporting role in a soup or a stew, or can be used to baffle the outsider who never saw one before. As individual products, both merlitons and satsumi are complete. Their charm as foods is that they have a limited range, so their meanings are not diffused by corporate universality and vagueness. They hold their shape because they aren't everywhere.

But put them together, and you see them at war with the cookbook cover. No cookbook cover would dare to establish this particular relationship between satsumi and merliton. In the first place, they are culinarily incompatible. They are practically incongruous as much as they are formally related. But even their formal relation is unconventional. The oranges and the squash are attracted to one another because Weiskopf's agenda is creolization. She has decided—for political reasons—to make sexy a New Orleans reality that is, de facto, sexy, but conventionally dangerous.

An art critic would never mention such grossly political notions in the presence of Weiskopf's obviously formal universe. But herein lies one of the ironic pleasures of her art. While this painting clearly draws its spectator to the virtuosity of her brushes and to the painterly world that references itself without seeming concern for narrative, there are yet intentions that call for non-art-historical comment and stories. It's not a guessing game either: Like any serious art, this painting operates on several levels. To the specialist, it is a cornucopia, one can expand the whole range of a critical vocabulary on it. But to the outraged food critic and to the carnal spectator, it represents an opportunity to throw fruit at the enemy.

(The enemy is boredom.)

The Heracliteans: Early Devils

I am of the school that says life isn't worth beans if something interesting doesn't happen every few hours. This school is ancient: Heraclitus and Sappho both belonged to it, but there is little or no record of it because the school abolished itself many times over the course of history and the Platonists destroyed all references to it. Plato and his gang were from the other school, which maintained that if *anything* interesting happened, it was a disaster bound to alter everything for the worse. The only things that happened, according to them, happened a long time ago and everything after that was anticlimactic.

We Heracliteans beat up on the Platonists whenever we see them skulking around the agora: The only drawback after that excitement is that tedium returns. We swing between tedium and terror but have some terrific moments in-between. Take yesterday in Tulsa: I met the manager of a drugstore photo shop who pointed out an old man leaning on a knobby cane before a rack of hunting magazines. "Yesterday," the photo manager said, "he brought in a stack of 1920s photographs of ballerinas. I asked him about it and he said that he was the artistic director of the Kirov Ballet in the twenties. He lives in one room in a flophouse now with all these pictures and God knows what else."

The photo manager paused as we both contemplated the awesomeness of that "God knows what else." Knobby canes, silk scarves, Trotsky's billets-doux, brittle locks of hair inside tarnished gold medallions, frayed slippers, crumbling flowers, a whole skeleton perhaps, belonging to the greatest ballerina of all time, the sad nineteen-year-old Lillova who disappeared without a trace one day. . . . All this time, the old man leaned perfectly still before the magazine rack, as if posing for our fantasies. "He's waiting for his pictures," the photo manager said, "it will be another two hours but he won't let them out of his sight." I thought about waiting for two hours too, but I already had my pictures.

Part Three

The Devil in

Eastern Euope, One of

His Ancestral Homes

Romania: The Varkolak

Well, it happened again. Everyone on the airplane was speaking Romanian. The blindingly blond Germans in front of me. The two French businessmen with identical crew cuts. The British captain. The Austrian stewardess. The American girls with Bibles returning from having collected souls in Bucharest. The satchel full of souls was under the seat in front of them. How was it possible? If they are speaking Romanian, I told myself reasonably enough, why don't I understand what they are saying? Well, actually, I *did* understand what they were saying, only it was not sensical. They spoke in bursts of poetry, in streams of oddly jumbled words. This happened to me once before when I went to Romania to cover the revolution: I came back hearing people speak sudden words in Romanian, a kind of code stuck by the secret police into the speech patterns of unsuspecting foreigners. Anyway, this time it was different. There is no revolution going on, and the secret police are too busy devouring themselves to bother much with echolalic philology. There were only two possible explanations: There is a little bit of Romanian in every Latin-based language, including English, and my reconditioned ear was picking it up. Or, *every* language is really Romanian and it is only the funny faces that people make which makes it come out in English or French or whatever. I may be speaking Romanian right now, for instance, and it is only your familiarity with my rhythms that makes you think I'm somewhat understandable. Be that as it may, it was not until I landed in Atlanta that the world reassumed its proper sound. But even if it hadn't, there is really nothing wrong with it. The world could do worse than to speak Romanian: It's a gentle, poetic, and generous language. After a week there, I felt quite inspired. The souls collected by the evangelical girls in the satchels in the seat in front of them babbled to each other in low murmurs. When released, they would doubtlessly teach everyone this dulcet Latin tongue.

Return to Romania:
Notes of a Prodigal Son

THE FIRST THREE TIMES: 1989, 1990, 1996

Each of my returns to Romania, since the first, in those heady days of December 1989, has been radically different. I have stayed reasonably the same but my compatriots have not, and to the extent that they have changed, they have granted me a new identity each time.

That first time, two days after the Ceauşescus were murdered, I went back as a journalist but also as a pilgrim in search of my lost childhood. I'd left at nineteen, in 1965, and I'd come back a grown man. Upon leaving, my mother and I had been made to sign papers renouncing our Romanian citizenship. In 1989, an American, I interviewed scores of people bursting with euphoria, wallowing in rivers of unbound speech after years of silence, caution, and fear. Thanks to the powerful news organizations I was representing, I had access to all the transitional figures of the new powers, as well as to the dissidents basking in the limelight of victory. It didn't take long, a few days at most, to realize that many of the new figures were not so new, and that the victorious dissidents were as divided from each other and from reality as they had always been. Thus, new became "new," and the revolution became "the revolution."

In my birth city of Sibiu, in Transylvania, where buildings were still burning as we made our way in, I met one of my old high-school friends, Ion V. He was an editor at *Tribuna*, the communist paper, which was then in the process of changing its name, like most institutions in Romania, hoping by this cosmetic maneuver to give an impression of real change. Ion fed me lavishly in his home, and then, at midnight, he drove me through the frozen streets of Sibiu, back to my hotel. On the way, we stopped in front of the building housing *Tribuna*. Ion asked me to wait in the car while he went in to get the next day's edition of the newspaper. I waited alone in his Dacia, hunched low in the front passenger seat, overwhelmed by a not-so-unreasonable fear. My colleagues were all in Bucharest, while the situation in the country was still far from settled. The Ceauşescus were dead but reports of fighting persisted. Authority in Sibiu was uncertain: the army was conducting arrests, looking for "terrorists," and sporadic shooting was still heard. As I waited for Ion, a man went running as fast as he could past the car, pursued by two civilians with drawn guns. Ion took a very long time. When he returned at last, after more than an hour, he was drawn and tense. He'd had to wait, he said, for the printers to finish the paper. I had the impression, however, that he had been discussing me with his superiors. My paranoid sixth sense told me that I had come very close to being either killed or arrested, and that Ion had been arguing on my behalf. I have never felt more like an exile, an American and a Jew, in my life. Whatever the essence of the argument, I am certain that one side had argued for my extinction on the grounds that the enemy of the moment was the foreigner, in the form of returning émigrés, the CIA, the KGB, and the Western media. Ion, however, was far from sure that he'd "won," and he advised me to be careful. In the following days, Securitate reorganized along nationalist lines, birthing such entities as "Vatra Romaneasca," whose stated enemies were, you guessed it, Jews, émigrés, the Western media, foreigners. Ion was clearly a sympathizer, if not a founder, but I was his friend.

I returned in June of 1990, ostensibly for our twenty-fifth high-school "reunion," an event that had quotation marks around it from the very beginning. A few days before, the so-called miners of the "new" Iliescu regime had beaten and killed students in University Square in Bucharest, where they had been protesting inside a self-declared "neo-communist free zone." This event, known as the "mineriada," lost Romania whatever capital of goodwill it had accrued during the December "revolution," revealing to the world the true nature of this "revolution," which had been nothing but a Securitate coup d'état. After the flood of negative publicity, Romania was desperately in need of good press.

My reception, this time, was outlandishly generous. On hand to record our high-school gathering were news teams from NPR and ABC's *Nightline*. (This was, of course, a hook for a story on the situation in Romania, not my personal press corps.) Ion handled the details of the "reunion" like a patriotic event. Unfortunately, the "reunion" was able to draw only four of my former colleagues, and their overly cautious spouses. The rest of our classmates, I was told, had either left the country, were unavailable or sick, or had died. This is not inconceivable, because the black-hole decades of the seventies and the eighties had indeed decimated Romanians in that fashion. But of the four remaining colleagues, I recognized only two. I don't have the greatest memory and I didn't harbor much affection for my high-school days or my classmates.

I will not go as far as to say that the two unknown ones were clones or replicas, but this conclusion would not have been untenable. Our discussions were political, charged, and barely civil. They were all defenders of Iliescu's brutality against the students. I felt on the other side of a huge gap that resembled, to put it charitably, the gap between students and government in 1968 in America. I had been on the side of students then and I was on the side of students now. My own generation, in Romania, had turned into the establishment, while I'd stayed the course. But this is, as I've said, charitable, because there were darker aspects to the whole business. For our party at the Emperor of the Romans Hotel, my friends had hired a folk band. With all their holiday-dressed families present, the occasion began quite festively. Soon, however, the happy drinking songs turned into nationalist anthems. One by one, the Hungarians and Germans in the hotel restaurant got up and left in protest. But some other tables of Romanians joined in the singing. Once more, I was being exempted. I was, true enough, a Jew, a foreigner, a Western newsman, but I was forgiven. In the name of childhood, of youth, of poetry, of fame, and the national self-interest, I was temporarily granted citizenship.

The third time I returned, in the spring of 1996, was to scout locations for a movie based on my mother's life, and to receive the literature prize of the Romanian Cultural Foundation. With me was Ted Thomas, my cowriter and director. We had hoped to make this a low-key visit, but fate intervened once more to make the visit timely. The prize-giving ceremony was in itself a political event, because the foundation prizes were all given to émigrés who had made names for themselves abroad. President Iliescu was conspicuously absent but former prime minister Petre Roman, now an opposition leader, was just as conspicuously present. Clearly, two competing political realities had begun to coexist. The strongly pro-Western faction led by Roman was making a stand against Iliescu's pro-Russian gorbachovists.

It appeared that I was doomed to return at historical moments. Of course, I'd missed numerous "historical" moments, but this one was, as it turns out, genuine, *sans* quotes. The most important election since 1989 was in progress. In the Bucharest apartment of my friends Denisa Comanescu and Nae Prelipceanu, I watched as their friend Victor Cioarba won the mayoralty of Bucharest against Iliescu's candidate, the tennis player Ilie Nastase. This was a referendum on Iliescu and it signaled the end of the crypto-communist status quo in Romania. Cioarba subsequently became prime minister in the Constantinescu cabinet, the first noncommunist, freely elected post-December Romanian government.

The day of the evening when we watched the returns on television, Ted and I had gone to polling places to watch the voting. The feeling in the country, even among that class of "average" people I had some contact with, mainly taxi drivers and voters at the polls, was one of cautious optimism. Romanians are effusive people, but even their greatest enthusiasms are tempered by an intrinsic knowledge of history, which has been rarely kind to them. The tension between the hopefulness necessary for going on and the organic knowledge of historical failure resolves itself in black humor and irony. Those qualities are the ingredients of survival, straws to cling to after the inevitable disappointments. Still, I felt a genuine belief that the new pro-Western leaders would alleviate the miserable economy with its insane inflationary spiral. The appropriate joke was that a man waits for his date in a coffee shop. She is late. When she appears, he says: "I've been waiting for you since coffee was two thousand lei."

My friends in Sibiu were quite crestfallen after the elections. One of them, Titi Ancuta, had actually run for mayor of that city on the neo-communist ticket and had been soundly defeated. The election had also been a rejection of the nationalist ideology that animated Ion V. and his shadow friends. Without Iliescu, the nationalist side was lost. This time, my stay at the Emperor of the Romans was marked mainly by sincere questions from my friends about business opportunities. Titi wondered about the marketing of a ski resort. My friends' depression about the waning nationalist cause had not lasted long because it'd been mainly political rhetoric, useful for holding on to the power they had accumulated during Ceaușescu's own brand of national-socialism. With renewed energy, Titi and the others were making a quick study of the rhetoric of business before throwing themselves wholeheartedly into the inevitable enterprise that now went by the name of "capitalism." My friends were, happily for them, a little slower and more wary than some of the hard-core Ceaușescu "formers" who had been weathering the transition in Bucharest by stealing everything that wasn't nailed down and "investing" it in scores of new businesses, including nightclubs, restaurants, strip joints, car dealerships, and property abroad. I didn't quite know the dimensions of this at the time. This discovery was reserved for my fourth visit.

THE FOURTH TIME (DIMENSION): 1997

My fourth visit resembled none of the others. This time, I was treated like returning royalty, the full-court press accorded the prodigal son. Romania had turned officially West. A massive effort to secure entrance into NATO had given the country a new public image that resulted in numerous recognitions, though the invitation to join NATO was not among them. The Constantinescu government appeared on the verge of genuine economic reform. Thieving officials of the Iliescu regime, with their Securitate shadows, were being indicted, prosecuted, and jailed. An acute panic appeared to possess the newly rich class of communists-turned-capitalists who'd started using their ill-gotten gains too brashly. I am still using qualifiers here because, despite the observers' hopes that Romania may finally be exiting its eternal quotation marks, this is just wishful thinking. One may consider these quotation marks as a set of permanent historical handcuffs or leg chains.

Romania can be seen now as the contentious space of a number of microcosms. The most obvious microcosm greets the visitor at Otopeni Airport, a Ceaușescu-era showpiece in the bad taste of the megalomaniac, who nearly bankrupted the country building horrid monuments to himself. There is no difficulty in entering the country now because visas and searches have been dispensed with. On exiting, however, one runs into a variety of unwholesome practices. Romanian money cannot be returned without an exchange slip, and then at considerable depreciation. The two coffeehouses where it is possible to spend the remainder of one's worthless lei charge five dollars a cup of coffee, which at 7,000 lei for a dollar amounts to a sack full of lei. The customs officers, with the same dour looks they've worn since their boss was snuffed, check the contents of suitcases and object mightily to baubles they choose to call "the national patrimony." Unless, of course, a bribe is quickly proffered. Otopeni is a bad gateway to the country, proof that public relations is in its infancy if it exists at all. Another explanation is that the border police are owned by one of the many opposition parties that make up the legislature. This one happens to be of the old stripe.

I was no casual visitor. A chauffeured van belonging to the foundation waited for me, as did three distinguished writers I am very fond of: the foundation president, Augustin Buzura, a revered Romanian novelist whose texts are in every high-school book; his assistant, the poet and novelist Carmen Firan, a spirited and beautiful woman with a long career of political public relations; and my wonderfully crazy publisher, Leonard Oprea (Nardi), whose unleashed style may be the freest form of foolishness in contemporary Romania.

I was quartered at the Elizabetha Palace, where the resignation of King Michael took place in 1947 under pressure from the Soviet-installed puppet communist government. The Elizabetha Palace, like Otopeni Airport, was another microcosm. Situated in a huge park next to the Museum of the Peasant, it had been built in the 1920s for the sad Princess Elizabetha who didn't speak a word of Romanian, wept a lot, and wrote bad poetry. The proportions were all wrong: Vast rooms with curved ceilings and flagstone floors ended in immense doors carved with royal crests that gave unto other immense rooms and empty courtyards. The staff, invisible most of the time, clustered in dark side rooms with cell phones. "The boys" were not exactly waiters but they did bring coffee when requested, forgetting the sugar for which they had to run kilometers down the halls. After bringing the sugar, they ran back the same distance to bring spoons. The telephone did a crazy dance of lights, which, according to the operator, "just happened." In the not-so-distant past, the palace had been some sort of top secret meeting place for the high ranks. Now, it appeared I was the only guest, but later I did see some rather disoriented Americans having meetings with local businessmen in various salons. Deer and peacocks grazed in the park outside the window.

The official function that was the purpose of my visit centered around the launching of my book of selected poems called *Alien Candor,* as well as the publication in Romanian of my book about the "revolution," *The Hole in the Flag.* The poems had been published by the Romanian Cultural Foundation in a deluxe bilingual edition, with a rapidity that was certainly novel in Romania. Under Augustin Buzura's friendly but firm pressure, my translator, the poet Ioana Ieronim, had put into Romanian over two hundred difficult poems in less than four weeks. The book editor, Carmen Firan, had worked days and nights for two weeks to finish the book. The reason for such haste had been to create a volume in honor of my fiftieth year, and because I was already in Prague and could easily come to Romania, thus saving the foundation plane fare. There was another reason, having to do with the political necessity of showing the West the friendliest possible face. I am not exaggerating my importance here, for the simple reason that Romania has few well-known names in the United States. Ilie Nastase had been compromised by his association with Iliescu. Nadia Comaneci had made a big fool of herself when she'd defected to America on the eve of the "revolution." Other exports were known only in high art circles, people like Andrei Serban and Liviu Ciulei, world-class theater directors. That left me, with an audience of twelve million people on National Public Radio. This was realpolitik, perfectly understandable. But there was also genuine concern for what Buzura called "the reintegration of true cultural values," which is a nearly transcendent concern, and which resounds to the credit of Romania's cultural stature. Despite the cynicism, the poverty, and the politics, Romanians are lovers of art and literature. It may be impossible (and unnecessary) to separate art from politics in a country where national consciousness has been forged by poets for the last three centuries. This was the reason also why the publication of a handsome volume of poetry counted more than the publication of my (still-dangerous) political memoir, *The Hole in the Flag,* or of my essay, "The Disappearance of the Outside," which had appeared the previous year.

The ceremony took place in the foundation's stately main hall where a standing-room-only audience of over two hundred invited luminaries, spanning the range from writers to President Constantinescu's chief councillor, Zoe Petre, crowded to hear speeches by the country's chief literary critic (and unsuccessful presidential candidate) Nicolae Manolescu; the dissident poet and my friend, Dorin Tudoran; and the foundation president, Augustin Buzura. The media were out in force, from radio to television and news dailies. The speeches were long and the crowd polite. "Why are speeches so long in this country?" I later asked Buzura. "If they are not, nobody thinks it's serious," he said. He was serious.

Carmen Firan, in the hope of lightening up the solemn affair, had engaged the services of a popular satirical rock group called Sarmalele Reci (Cold Stuffed Cabbage). The band was not allowed, however, to perform their repertoire; they were asked to play jazz, which they did very well. The speeches, except for Dorin Tudoran's warm and personal essay, were over the top in my estimation. They called me "great" so many times I began fantasizing that Romania might be my back door to the Nobel Prize. After the speeches, I sat down to sign books and was attacked by the media. While most people waited patiently in line, the "important" guests broke in quite rudely, often dragging in someone else important I just "had to meet."

A LITTLE DIGRESSION

The queue is a fundamental microcosm. It is composed of people who have no choice but to wait. In other words, "the people," as politicians are fond of calling them. The people, in all lands and times, wait. My acquaintances and their acquaintances were all "important" and never worried about the patient folk who gritted their teeth but said nothing. They took it for granted that "the important" had priority. The American in me was embarrassed for the crowd's eternal patience. Why didn't anybody raise a fuss? Here was the result of forty years of communism, two decades of fascism, and countless years of masters and serfs: no respect for the rights of the seemingly unconnected. It was no trivial matter. Lines are the historical form of most social activity in Romania. For most of their history, Romanians stood in line for food, for amusement, for news, for recognition. Individually and nationally, Romanians have been the most patient line-standers in Europe. Historically, this patience was rewarded by the abrupt closing of the window just when they got to the front. Others, better "connected," had gotten there first. Slowly, the idea that fairness is not rewarding must have seeped into the national psyche.

It may seem a lot to make out of an occasion that was after all "mine," it may even be ungrateful, but nearly thirty years in America have instilled in me a physical allergy at such infringement on humble rights. Ironically, this exacerbated sense of an individual's worth was a reaction born in Romania, where I seethed throughout my adolescence whenever an official claimed priority by dint of "importance." For years, I saw red (to coin a phrase) whenever anyone in uniform, from policemen to school principals, stepped on what I believed to be my rights. This attitude continued in America, which is not as free of bullying by uniforms as one might like to think. Until such simple ideas as respect for the line are widely in use, there is little hope for what we glibly call "democracy." Of course, this may be a European, not an exclusively Romanian problem. Leaving Romania, at the Otopeni Airport, a couple of Frenchmen tried to get right in front of me with their luggage cart. By this time I'd had it, and I really enjoyed telling them to fuck off and wait in line like everybody else.

The "democracy" being invented in Romania is also defined by the new media, which were pushing and shoving to get ahead of itself and of everybody else to get what they wanted, in this case my "attention." In the service of democracy, the free press was ready to trample everyone. In this respect, at least, Romanian journalists had caught up quickly to their Western counterparts. Foreign forms of rudeness were being imported to supplement the native ones.

THE RESTAURANTS

It is said that Romanians are francophiles and, in one respect, they are. They accord the utmost importance to restaurants, restaurateurs, chefs, and waiters. The very definition of Being Somebody is contingent on having one's own restaurant, personally knowing the *patronul*, being known to the waiters. The expensive restaurants and clubs in Bucharest are another microcosm. Owned by well-heeled, well-connected figures with a spotted if not downright shady past, these establishments collect Important Figures just as the IFs collect them.

After the ceremony, a distinguished company of foundation officials and their important friends, including former Culture Minister Andrei Plesu, artist Tudor Jebeleanu, and feared political columnist Elena Stefoi, gained entry to a splendidly appointed establishment. I had made the faux pas of inviting my childhood friend N.S. and his wife to join the august company. There was no complaint from my gracious hosts. N.S. and wife—he is a poet, she an artist and translator—are quite humble people, but neither their reputation nor their appearance meshed with the group's. This is not to say that anyone harbored uncharitable impulses: They were cordial. But reservations had been made, the place was inordinately expensive, and the private room where we were seated had been strictly arranged to accommodate the reservation. After some quite serious grumbling by the maître d', tables were rearranged to fit us all. When everyone was seated, the *patronul* appeared and started to rage, delivering an extraordinary political speech. From what I was able to ascertain he accused the current administration—of which this crowd was clearly part—of destroying the aesthetic of his restaurant, something that previous governments, including that of the executed couple, had never been guilty of. The company, which began listening with amused twitters to the eccentric *patronul*, sobered up as he went on, falling into an awkward silence. The man was briefly stopped when a tactful Carmen Firan offered him a copy of my book, which I hastily signed. Unfortunately, he resumed and would have gone on if Andrei Plesu, with the brutal but perfectly appropriate gesture of a man of authority, hadn't stopped him with these words: "And surely, your wife doesn't love you either."

It was the perfect thing. The food was great, the smoke thick, the conversation witty, charged, and as laden with irony and double entendres as an oxen cart filled with Transylvanian hay. But while repartee set the general tone, small fires burst here and there. Dorin Tudoran brought up, with characteristic seriousness, the matter of Securitate and its still-visible shadow. The unresolved murder of Professor Ioan Coulianou in Chicago by what Dorin and I both believe were officers of Securitate took on the form of a serious argument. The natives preferred to believe that Securitate, for all its vaunted pervasiveness, was an outfit of bumblers and ninnies.

There were other restaurants. The first night, Augustin Buzura and Carmen Firan played host at a sweet, old-fashioned garden restaurant called La Gogoase (At the Doughnuts), owned by the mother of an expatriate who had returned from Chicago to cook (splendidly) the national food. We had stuffed cabbage with *mamaliga, mititei*, and fabulous supa de *peris oare*.

Next night, after many drinks and hors d'oeuvres at my friend Ďenisa Comanescu's house, we headed (with two other guests of Denisa's: a Swedish poet and a pretty Romanian translator) to a rendezvous with my friend Ioan T. Morar at another fancy garden restaurant and club. Ioan was there with his wife and son, a brilliant young boy who spoke perfect English. He'd told me before to try to come accompanied only by Nardi, my publisher, but as always in these circumstances, my bohemian instincts tend to think such instructions unimportant. I like crowds and enjoy rolling on while picking up playmates. When we all showed up, Ioan was most gracious and disapproval was, once more, expressed only by the *patronul*, who made it plain that he didn't expect so many people. I have no fear of the food sector, but then I'm American, which is to say, I can always go somewhere else. Ioan is an immensely popular writer and television personality but the *patronul* cowed him a little nonetheless.

Ioan T. Morar is also an editor at *Academia Catavencu*, a savagely funny satirical weekly that had been the target of SRI (Securitate's successor) several times. Its offices were bugged, its writers threatened. In addition to unveiling with remarkable candor a myriad of dirty deeds by the mighty and their underlings, *Academia Catavencu* had also the distinction of stealing the mass readership of the nationalist hate weekly, *Romania Mare*. What the switch in allegiance showed was that the Romanian masses craved passionate opposition more than ideology. *Catavencu* combines satire with hard-hitting scandal, while *Romania Mare* specializes only in scandal and incitement to murder. One might draw here the conclusion that Romanians are closer to the peripatetic Sweikian humor of *Catavencu*, than to the murderous stupidity of the Iron Guard. But one can argue equally that Romanians are composed of two sides that do not know one another, existing in separate incendiary compartments: a self-deprecating, tolerant side, and a pompous, sentimental one.

MONEY & GOODS

All the exclusive eateries charged American prices: Each tab for these meals came to several hundred dollars, which in Romania is plain obscene. A tenured university professor makes $150 a month, while a skilled working man can count on about $30. How anyone survives is a mystery. The prices on the free markets in Bucharest are very high, as are the prices for clothes and shoes. Yet the city had plenty of elegant people, and all the restaurants were full. On the boulevards of Bucharest, once trafficked exclusively by the locally made Dacia cars, there were plenty of Oldsmobiles, Jeeps, and BMWs. Armani-suited young men with cellular phones and rail-thin model-type girlfriends swarmed the Calea Victoriei, the still-elegant though grimy main street, where the casinos and the Western-style shops are. It would be all too easy to call all these types "the new Mafia," or "the new businessmen," depending on your tolerance, but many of them seemed to be just stylish young students. I thought about stopping one couple to ask them in detail the price of their duds, hoping to analyze the data in the manner of Guy Davenport's in-depth look at the famous painting *American Gothic*. I didn't have the nerve, but the mystery preoccupied me.

I got an unexpected clue when I saw the Cultural Foundation budget lying on Augustin Buzura's desk while I was giving a phone interview in his office. It was ridiculously small. The gala night's meal would have cost about half of the annual budget. Yet the foundation was well staffed by bright, multilingual women and men, and it employed several chauffeurs with well-maintained cars. The explanation I was given was that the foundation budget came from the Ministry of the Exterior and that it was subject to supplemental funds when needed. Augustin Buzura was also a tireless fundraiser who personally solicited businesses for aid. While this explained how the foundation got by, everyone else, it seemed, had access to supplemental funds that were more mysterious. Given that a professional's average monthly salary was about fifty dollars per month, it was hard to see how my friends survived. I glimpsed the existence of a vast underground economy, the presence of unspoken budgets, possible through an immensely complicated web of personal connections. The country's elites were linked and the links had been created, enforced, and reinforced in the very restaurants of the powerful *patronii*.

The existence of this underground must be plain as day to anyone involved, but to me it was shocking. I am not naive. The underground economies of Eastern Europe and Russia have been well documented by both the local press and international media. I knew that the most obvious new capitalists were smart old communists who transferred state property to private use. But I'd believed, on the basis of the lofty ideas about "democracy" being debated in the better forums, that the nation was honestly striving to build a civil society based on frank and open exchange. The former dissidents, now in positions of responsibility, had been the keepers of a moral discourse of such purity it shamed those of us in the West who, like most people, try to get by as best we can. Recall Václav Havel's extraordinary speech to both houses of Congress in 1993. He mentioned God, integrity, philosophers, and

Western civilization, notions so alien to our political discourse, it made the worst cynics weep. And yet here were people, not quite Havels but still, who were plainly part of a *modus vivendi* that belied such loftiness. From their inability to wait in line to their paper budgets, the keepers of the moral discourse played the game.

My new vision of the underground was that it was *total*. There was no one in the whole country who was not somehow involved. How could they survive otherwise? The stated paper earnings of most people were below subsistence levels.

So radical a vision can be rightly called paranoiac if I hadn't had plenty of occasions to see the banal reality of much of my previous paranoias. When I'd called "the revolution" a coup d'état there were still plenty of believers. When I suspected my old high-school chums of secret connections, I'd had little proof. Later, they admitted it freely. But my paranoia is not the point. As I was to find out, paranoias much greater than mine flourished in the minds of most individuals I encountered, including, to my regret, some of my very best friends. I would be committing hubris to think that my paranoias are somehow more realistic than theirs. Still, the paranoia of an outsider and the *tissue* of paranoias that make up the psychic life of a nation are quite different things.

LEONARD OPREA (NARDI)

The exhausting round of galas and festivities in Bucharest would have quickly taken its toll if it hadn't been for the sweet madness of Nardi who, while paranoid like most Romanians, acted as if he were entirely free to speak his mind. Nardi crossed himself every time we passed a church but had a Jewish grandmother and a Jewish wife, and was, on top of everything, interested in Indian spirituality and the occult. This was by no means unique: A staggering amount of superstition possessed every Romanian in some form. Forty years of dialectical Marxism had done no more than to create believers in astrology, amulets, and the occult.

In Nardi's case, all this took on the form of continual questioning and an earnest enthusiasm for the life of the mind. While quite merciless in his appraisal of people, including some of our good friends, he assumed the presence of a higher reality in everyone and everything. The realistic level at which he operated was mitigated by an insane generosity and genuine love for fellow beings. Nardi's generosity was only proportionally greater than that of most Romanians, who exhibit a syndrome I once called "aggressive hospitality." The idea is to make continual gifts to friends and strangers, pick up every restaurant tab, give unlimited time and attention, and proffer any service whether possible or impossible. The fervor of this national mania may have equivalents only in the potlatch cultures of some Native Americans, but in those cultures there is at least the reasonable certainty that the beneficiaries of the exchange will eventually reciprocate. No such certainty attends the suicidal generosity of Romanians and, of all Romanians, Nardi's was the greatest. He fought to pay for everything, made me gifts of his most cherished possessions, and would have jumped off a cliff if he'd thought it would please me. This attitude was wholly bothersome to me until I understood, in Sibiu, that he couldn't help it.

SIBIU, THE FOURTH TIME AROUND

My hosts this time were not my high-school chums who had been relegated, because of local cultural politics, to playing second fiddle. The highly intellectual group that organized my books' "launching" in Sibiu consisted of the poets and artist editors of *Euphorion*, a smartly produced review of literature. Iustin Panta, Dumitru Chioaru, and Mircea Stanescu met me in the lobby of the Imparatul Romanilor, where I was already something of a celebrity. Mrs. Ionescu, the desk manager, was, as it turned out, a reader. She had consumed all my previously published work and was overjoyed when I presented her with signed copies of the new books. (By morning, she'd read everything, and got no sleep at all.) The *Euphorion* group may not have read as much as Mrs. Ionescu, but they came prepared with a tape recorder and notes.

The Emperor of the Romans Hotel, once a prewar Austrian style nightspot, was the very place where, my mother told me, my father had "wasted his youth on women and cards." The apple doesn't fall far from the tree, but the hotel in its present incarnation offered no such opportunities. Still, it was an elegant old place. The windows looked over the magical rooftops of Sibiu with their "sleepy eyes," and the current owner had renovated pleasantly but not excessively. The restaurant below had been the scene of my friends' past nationalist excess but was now full of German tourists who came in great numbers, though not nearly equal to the numbers of native Germans who'd emigrated from Sibiu after the "revolution."

My interviewers had one essential question. Was it possible for a Romanian artist-thinker to contribute coherently to the intellectual dialogue of the West? Have no fear, my friends, I told them. This was the most important thing I told them, though I continued. Have no fear, I said, of speaking your ideas into the vast din that is now the West's babble of discourses. Who you are and what you represent are sorely needed in a world soon to be possessed by a virtuality that makes surrealism a poor source of imagination. There is a place for you by virtue of your desire to participate and by the immense native talent that you have fed on. I cited the examples of Eugen Ionescu (no relation to the desk manager), E. M. Cioran, and Mircea Eliade, who had shaped substantial areas of Western discourse after the war. These writers, I said, brought to the table exactly what you might: the reservoir of an intellectual tradition that is still fresh. I meant these things. At the same time, they hinged on a heavy contingency, namely the business of "who you are and what you represent." Had I brought into play all I'd been thinking about the self-representations of current Romanians, I might have half offended them. I say "half," because the Euphorionites were not naive. They knew that their essays were rooted in the dilemmas of a society at odds with itself, a moral swamp from which "les fleurs du mal," if they were to take sublime forms, had to be obtained at the price of a new integrity. They knew also, or I hoped they did, that the moral contradictions embodied by such of their predecessors as Eliade and Cioran, were no longer tolerable. Cioran and Eliade had been fascists in their youth and, while Cioran had rejected this ideology resolutely, Eliade never had. Did they know this? And if they did, what did it mean to them?

On the night of the "launching" the room at the Student Cultural Center was filled with a chosen group of people. The only reason some of my old friends came was that Nardi, suspecting the *Euphorion* gang of elitism, had contacted the newspaper and the television station on his own. Word had barely gotten out. It hadn't been the group's intention to make this an open forum. When I found this out, I objected most strenuously. "My books," I said, "should be read by everyone. Besides, my friend Nardi here needs to make a buck to recoup his costs. Everyone you invited is getting free books." "Point well taken," exclaimed the director of the Student Center, Constantin Chiriac, "we could have leafleted the union halls and gotten thousands, but we wanted to keep it classy."

To understand just how twisted this reasoning was, you must know that "the masses," in whose name the communists had created their own elite, enjoy no more prestige in the post-communist era than they ever did. Opposition intellectuals who took up politics after "the revolution," who'd had to address the masses, did so against their deepest instincts. The contempt translated into the polls, hence the longevity of Iliescu's standstill government. Nicolae Manolescu, one of Romania's best critical thinkers, told me that a journalist had once come to interview him without having read any of his books. Imagine. The poor journalist. No wonder Manolescu lost so badly at the polls: Only ten voters had read his books.

Nonetheless, the evening was "a success," as my friends ceaselessly assured me. No matter what happened, how much psychological uneasiness had been produced, the main thing was to be "a success." The impulse to endow all events, even catastrophes, with a positive spin, is an unfortunate human, not uniquely Romanian, desire. The evening was not a catastrophe, but what did the "success" consist of? It consisted, no doubt, of a genius talk by the sage of Sibiu, the poet and translator Mircea Ivanescu. Wrapped like a cocoon in a silver-haired aura of civility, with Coke-bottom glasses that make his eyes look infinitely deep, Ivanescu, the translator into Romanian of James Joyce and Robert Musil, is the very heart of erudite civilization.

Listening to Ivanescu spin his weave of commentary on the margin of my poor poems, I had the absolute sense of the greatness of Romanian culture. Just as I had previously visioned (not *en*-visioned) the *total underground* of the Romanian economy, I now saw into its murky depths the ingot of pure gold that would save them all. Here was a man, a genius, but, perhaps more important, a scholar, for whom the life of the mind was absolute. The life of his body was as incidental as it is for any saint, because he emanated a simplicity of love that transcended matter. I could provide here the details of his life to prove this assertion, but it is wholly unnecessary. Saints are knowable directly, and if the facts support their sainthood, as they inevitably will, it's only because the pope's bureaucracy demands them. Believe me: Ivanescu is a saint. His living among the citizens of Sibiu, including the Euphorionites, is what makes it possible for them to be equal participants in European culture. I say this knowing full well that there are others like him in Romania, prima facie evidence of moral certainty. This would be a sordid story without them.

MY FRIENDS, THE FOURTH TIME AROUND

Titi was bursting with enthusiasm: after his unsuccessful run for mayor of Sibiu, he'd gone full tilt into business. He had built a commodity exchange, which he was dying to show me.

The Sibiu Commodity Exchange was a new building near the train station. It was airy and modern, with a wide marble staircase leading to an open meeting room. Titi employed twenty-five brokers with gleaming new computers. Four hundred companies were listed on the exchange. The exchange had opened just the past week, on 12 July 1997. On the desk in his spacious office with wall-sized windows overlooking the ancient spires of Sibiu was a stack of newspapers headlining the event.

"Unfortunately," Titi sighed, "your President Clinton stole the first page."

Not completely. News of Titi's exchange was just below the photograph of an open-mouth Clinton captured in midspeech and a toothy Emil Constantinescu caught, one supposes, in midthanks. "The First Futures Trading in Romania Organized on the Occasion of the Exchange's Official Opening!" trumpeted *Tribuna*.

I asked Titi how he'd managed this capitalistic coup. He was a trained veterinarian, a manager until 1989 of a pig farm. He told me an astonishing story. He had put an ad in a New York émigré newspaper seeking financial advice for the founding of a bank. A man of local origin, named Thomas Curtean, answered. Mr. Curtean was guru to numerous American financial institutions. He had written several primary texts about the functioning of brokerage institutions. He was also getting on in age, was nostalgic for his birthplace, and intended to buy, for sentimental reasons, the house where his parents were born. Titi and Curtean struck up a friendship that resulted in Curtean moving into Titi's house for several months and creating the exchange. Curtean trained Titi's brokers gratis, a job for which he normally charged hundreds of thousands of dollars, and supervised every aspect of the enterprise until it began to function.

"What are the laws regarding exchanges?" I asked.

"That's the beauty of it!" shouted Titi. "There aren't any!"

And, of course, since there weren't any, they would be written on the basis of a fait accompli. Titi was writing the laws. He was rightly proud of his initiative and full of enthusiasm for what his attitude portended. It meant that anyone with the nerve to seize the initiative (and with the necessary connections, naturally) could make a bundle in Romania. In this respect, Romania is where Poland, Hungary, or the Czech Republic were seven years ago.

Titi's enthusiasm was infectious. In addition to the exchange, he owned a factory for manufacturing meat products and had built a splendid set of apartments for lease to wealthy businessmen or consular residents. He hadn't given up his dream of a ski resort in the mountain village of Saliste and was bubbling with all kinds of other entrepreneurial ideas.

The gleaming new building of the Commodity Exchange contrasted most glaringly with the shabbiness of Sibiu's ancient historical district. Sibiu, a medieval city, is one of the jewels of Europe in terms of its architecture, history, and importance. Cornel Lungu, the director of the Bruckenthal Historical Museum, explained that no effort was being made either to preserve or to renovate the old city. There was a lack of political will, despite the fact that tourism, just trickling now, could revive the local economy.

Titi showed none of his characteristic enthusiasm when I asked him about it. The sorry state of the municipality was the fault of local government, he said, which refused to sell the historical buildings to private investors. Only such investors, backed by laws concerning preservation, could save the city. It was amazing to hear such resolute market ideas: Had so much time passed since 1989 when he'd been the director of a collectivist enterprise?

The business of Sibiu's crumbling architecture and the necessity to save it preoccupied me for the next two days. I brought up the problem with everyone, including my old friend Ion V., who was still an editor at *Tribuna* but seemed depressed. While his friend Titi was getting quickly rich, Ion had remained in place. He suggested the formation of a Codrescu Foundation to see to the old city's revival. This was more than my fragile ego could stand, and I was not about to lend myself to his sagging career.

Just how precarious Ion's standing in town was became evident after the "launching" of my book. Hoping to see all my old and new friends in one place, I suggested that we go eat and drink together. Here, however, I came up against the reality of Romania.

"If V. comes," one of the *Euphorion* editors said, "none of us will."

"But he's my friend," I insisted. "Can you tell me why?"

He did. It was a sordid story that had all the earmarks of gossip and no hard facts.

"Well, then," I told him, "I don't care if you come."

Meanwhile, Ion left mysteriously and promised to join us in the restaurant.

"We will go with you," said the *Euphorion* man, "but when V. comes we are all going to get up and leave."

The restaurant was of the *patronul* club variety, an immense space with linen tablecloths and a mirrored stage. The group ordered drinks and food, and we fell into an intense argument about past and present.

"Why don't you bring all your suspicions into the open?" I asked. "How long can you go on suspecting and hating people? It is paralyzing. Nothing can go on unless you forgive."

It wasn't so easy, they explained. "The formers" still had power, they were the newly rich and the still-powerful. To go against them was to risk persecution, just as in the old days. Better to devote oneself to rigorous intellectual activity, restrict oneself nobly to culture.

"But this is simply defeatism," I cried, with indignant American righteousness, "the press is free. You have the right to speak out. And if you really hate somebody, you can always hire a goon to break their legs."

During our discussion, and unbeknownst to me, a slew of strippers had appeared on the mirrored stage, courtesy of the *patronul*, who wished to maintain harmony and high-mindedness in his establishment. The only one who noticed the girls was also the only woman at the table, Iustin Panta's young girlfriend. She watched in fascinated silence, as the men thrashed in the cauldron of their anxieties.

PRESCRIPTIONS

"And what," bellowed the drunken Costica, "is the answer?"

"First," replied the equally drunk American-Romanian poet, "The currency must be changed to reflect reality. The lion (leu) must be replaced by the mosquito (tintarul)! Second, volunteer brigades of conflict-resolution counselors must descend on this country at once. And third, Prozac in the water!"

"All doable!" shouted the can-do Costica, causing the banquet table to jump and take a sudden leap across an invisible barrier, "but we cannot change the lion into a mosquito overnight!"

"Even if the facts require it?"

"*Especially* if the facts require it!"

This was progress. Originally, facts just simply didn't matter. Now they did because they had to be *defied*. Viva el progresso!

Ion V. never showed up.

THE DREAM

My last night in Romania I dreamt that I was traveling on a narrow road between two crumbling, ancient walls. These walls were extremely close together, but the road between them was cozy, fast, and soft. Traveling with me along this road were all the country's fat cats, intelligentsia, and nomenclatura together. People outside the walls had no idea that this road existed. When I emerged outside, I told several people casually that I'd just gotten off the underground road. They shrugged uncomprehending. I even pointed out to them the place in the wall where one could enter, but still they did not believe me. And yet the road exists. I knew it in my dream and I know it now. Romania is a country tunneled through and through by the cushy underground road, which is how anybody who's anybody gets from one point to another. The rest of the folk, the so-called people, stand in line in the hot sun, scratching their heads. They know that something's wrong, but they can't quite identify the rumbling sound under their feet and all around them. They are waiting in line for NATO to do something.

DOGS

At a party given by a Western advertising firm in a palace near Bucharest, among the tables laden with food and the sounds of an orchestra, the nouveaux riches mingled with politicos and writers. A group of us, which included two academicians who had landed on their feet throughout several changes of regime, their elegant young secretaries, and Radu Florescu, author of a book on Dracula, were taken across a field and shown the broken stones of a church demolished by Ceauşescu. It had been carted secretly and hidden here by cover of night. However, these sacred relics were not safe yet: some nouveaux riches were stealing the stones to bury them in the foundations of their new houses. Across the same field, lying on his back, was the huge statue of Lenin torn from its pedestal at the center of Bucharest. Under him was the slightly smaller statue of Petru Groza, Romania's first communist prime minister. Some of the irreverent young climbed on top of Lenin for pictures. Here was the new Romania: surreal, absurd, ironic, elegant, and still awed by the recent past. The Writers' Union, once the country's chief center of dissidence, is surviving on the profits of a casino it runs on a fashionable boulevard. The fashionable boulevards, as well as the side streets, are overrun by gentle dogs that became homeless during Ceauşescu's orgy of demolition in the eighties. Originally, the homeless dogs had been marked for destruction but the citizens protested. A Swiss animal rights group is now sterilizing them and letting them run free. The people of Bucharest feed them. No one knows how many wild dogs run the streets, but estimates range from forty to one hundred thousand. Truly wild dogs befriend pets safely ensconced behind fences: The sight of two or three wild dogs lying on the sidewalk outside a gate fraternizing with the dogs inside is quite common. When the pampered pets are taken for a walk by their owners, the wild friends trail behind with an air of pride meant to telegraph to the *truly* homeless dogs hidden in the bushes that they have a family, even if it's a tenuous, temporary one. This self-appointed second column of self-deluded dogs resembles nothing more than the masses of Romanian people who believe that Europe will eventually accept them into the Union, if only they had that general air of belonging.

Not all the wild dogs were as agreeable as the friends of the pets. One night, returning to the eerie Elizabetha Palace with Nardi, we ran into a pack of canines living in the woods adjoining the Museum of the Peasant. Facing the growling pack, I had an inexplicable flashback to a time when I hadn't even been born, namely the 1930s when groups of drunken fascists would accost innocent citizens, looking for Jews to beat up. I faced the dogs firmly and said, quite incongruously: "This is 1997! You can't just bite us!" Amazingly, they obeyed, retreating into the bushes. To this day, I am convinced that these were indeed fascists and that, in the country where the werewolf originated, such transformations are not all that unusual.

At the beginning of my visit, a woman from radio fought with one from TV over an interview with me. And two other TV stations waited outside, while paparazzi flashed. To the question, "How do you find Romania now?" I answered, "Like a cat caught in a door, halfway in and halfway out." I didn't know about the dogs yet.

The Berlin Mall

I spent a whole month in Prague observing the decade-old consuming appetites of post-communism. The Berlin Wall is becoming the Berlin Mall and there is no stopping it. I have observed the Czechs begin to submit slowly but willingly to the lures of advertising, the seduction of credit, and the pleasures of carting home objects they never knew they needed and that they have little use for. The victory of capitalism began in 1989 with the occupation of Prague's most significant corners by Coca Cola and McDonald's, our advance guard companies in all new markets. These companies underwent favorable mutations in the new territories because, unlike their American counterparts, they are the height of fashion. Young Czechs find it chic to be seen at McDonald's eating french fries that cost twice as much as the local equivalent. McDonald's is not cheap because, like blue jeans, it is still more of a religion than a restaurant, signifying membership in the (capitalist) future. Coca Cola has, of course, staked the skies and there is no looking up without seeing the logo. The skies in this case begin at the very top of your head because every café umbrella is Coke-scripted. Local attempts at capitalism are thriving, though the most successful ones distribute American or Asian clothes and electronics and serve purely as outlets for the raging river of goods flowing from across the ocean. To Czechs (and to Europeans in general) style is everything, so you won't quite find the ease of

Wal-Mart here because shopping hasn't yet become relaxation. To be observed shopping, to display your purchases, and to gloat over your possessions is part of the experience. The quintessential symbol of all these qualities is the cell phone, or should I say The Cell Phone in capital letters. Eastern Europeans have taken to the Cell Phone with the fervor that must have attended their religious conversions in history. To be slim, tailored, freshly barbered or coiffed, walking under the Coca Cola skies on your way to McDonald's, with the Cell Phone glued to your ear, speaking to your friends, is the Peak of Glam (as in Glamour). And what you are talking about to your friends or (best of all) to your country cousins is the fact that you are walking under the Coca Cola skies freshly barbered or coiffed on your way to . . . etc. Most likely you will be talking about this with other Cell Phone holders walking under similar Coke skies to . . . etc. And when you meet your date for the evening, she or he will be also holding a Cell Phone and you will munch your fries and drink your Coke while continuing to speak to others as fortunate as you (or not). The trouble is that not everyone is as fortunate as the Cell Phoners. In fact, few people can afford a cell phone, or even fries. The living wage in the Czech Republic is about one-twentieth that of Americans. A doctor makes about a hundred dollars a month, so you can be sure that such status symbols are the result of sacrifice and hard work. People on pensions can't even dream of such conveniences (if this is what they are) and you can see them scurrying to cheap markets holding plastic bags inscribed with advertising for things they will never have.

The only limit to the triumph of capitalism is transportation. Happily, public transportation still prevails over automobiles. In Prague, buses, subways, and electric trams do a superb job of carrying weary shoppers home. This civilized service is a legacy of deceased socialism and, while people take it for granted, they would be miserable without it. The beauty of public transport is that you cannot haul more goods home than you can carry. Therefore, you cannot shop until you drop. People with cars have more room to carry things and, while some people have small cars, few of them have station wagons or trucks. Americans could take home the material contents of entire Czech villages if ever they happened upon them. Luckily, they haven't yet, but you can be sure that a river of station wagons and trucks is massing quietly outside the borders of Eastern Europe, waiting for just the right moment to invade. Small European countries are hypersensitive about their history, which consists mostly of invasions and takeovers. In the past, these invasions were easy to spot because the enemy wore uniforms and their cars had machine guns mounted on them. The new occupation forces are friendly though, and give you (seemingly) pleasure instead of pain. So far, the population is welcoming the invaders with flowers and excitement. What they will do when they wake up poor, in debt, and laden with defunct electronics cannot yet be guessed. There is no known antidote to consumerism yet. This invasion may be permanent.

Prague (cont.)

Prague is a gawker's paradise. The old Austro-Hungarian empire and the kingdoms before it left behind some mighty structures. Knowing their history puts a certain edge on their ornaments since it consists mainly of bloody episodes. For a thousand years, people were regularly thrown out of windows for political reasons in Prague, a process known as "defenestration," and if the cobblestones were not spattered by falling bodies, there were plenty of hangings, burnings, and barricade-making to mark them. Today's tourists think that they are in Disneyland because the restoration of Prague has gone to fairy-tale colors, and fairy tales, as everyone knows, have happy endings. In fairy tales, the bad dragons get their heads chopped off and the hero gets to live with the heroine in a castle. The tourists may not know it, but there are still some bad dragons in the Czech Republic today and some of them reside right in the castle, which is ruled by Kafka's ghost and President Havel's reputation.

The situation of the Gypsies or Romanys is one of the quiet demons stalking the Czech fairy tale. During the Nazi occupation of Czechoslovakia, thousands of them were deported to a concentration camp at Leti where brutal guards murdered most of them. They drowned babies in the lake and shot pregnant women and children. The Czechs have long maintained that German nazis had run the Leti camp. But it turns out that the butchers of

Leti were Czech, not German, and nobody in the Republic, including the president, wants to wake up *that* ghost.

Paul Polanski, a Czech-American who lives in Prague, has made it his life mission to draw attention to that horror and to interview the Leti survivors. Unfortunately, the Leti massacres are not just relevant history, but a direct link to the situation of Czech gypsies today. Over thirty Gypsies have been murdered by skinheads since 1989, with only one conviction to date. There have been hundreds of attacks with injuries by racists and neo-Nazis. Graffiti with messages like "Send Gypsies to the camps," appear regularly.

Paul Polanski has lived with Czech Gypsy families and knows their misery firsthand. Unemployed, shunned, and poor, these proud people have a complex and rich culture, marked by living generously, delighting in storytelling, music, and fine craftsmanship. Their chief crime is their skin color. Polanski boiled down their long and intricate stories to a series of brisk, factual poems that speak tersely of an entire culture. The publication of his book was greeted with criticism and disbelief in the Czech Republic. The message from the castle was: shut up! The Leti camp received an official monument thanks to Polanski's efforts, but he was not invited to the opening ceremonies.

Prague is indeed a mighty city, but the shadows of her aesthetic delights are long and deep.

I was eating my first salad in Eastern Europe at Kampa Park under the Charles Bridge in Prague, when a gaggle of Secret Service agents burst into the restaurant escorting Madeleine Albright. "Thank you," I heard her say, "for finding a place so late." Next day, I read in the *Herald-Tribune* that she'd been in St. Petersburg earlier and was in the Czech Republic to receive a medal from President Havel in gratitude for her role in bringing NATO to the Czechs. Meanwhile, the waiter was grinning from ear to ear: "She's Czech, you know." "I know. She's also Jewish," I said. "Yes, yes," said the waiter, "but she didn't know it."

I threw some bread to the oversized swans in the Vltava River and looked at the lights of Prague, this amazing jumble of Gothic, baroque, Cubist and commie buildings, which is now the new Paris of Europe and, thanks to NATO, the new border of Western Europe. When the Iron Curtain lifted, Prague was the gleaming jewel that sat in the debris pile of Eastern European cities. The commies didn't have the money, or perhaps the heart, to wreck it.

Next day I went to the old Jewish Quarter, five hundred years of ghetto history crowded in the stones of a small cemetery. The remains of the Golem, a human being created and then destroyed by Rabbi Leow in the sixteenth century, lay under lock and key in the attic of the Old Synagogue. Legend has it that the rabbi made the Golem to defend the Jews from their persecutors. The Nazis so enjoyed this tale, they planned to transform the Jewish Quarter into what they called "The Museum of an Extinct Race." They didn't finish the job, so the Jew Franz Kafka is now the city's most visible citizen. And the Jews who comprised the famed Prague Circle in the 1920s are among the world's best-known philosophers. I sat in the Franz Kafka café, across from the house where he was born, and watched some of the twenty thousand expatriate writers who, I was told, live in Prague now, strut by with alchemical incunabula under their arms. Some of them were doubtlessly Jews, giving Central Europe back its missing spirit, though they probably didn't know it. It is said that the number of expats is equal to the number of sexy, recently degrimed gargoyles that stare down from Prague's gleaming new façades. The ancient alchemists of Rudolf the Second were just as numerous before Rudolf threw them into the castle moat, where they were eaten by bears. The expats are safer, though, with a playwright in the castle, the Republic in NATO, and the dollar worth about thirty five crowns, which will buy your starving artist two glasses of flaming absinthe and a plate of boar stew in a *pivnice*. I mean, it's a fine day when bohemians can actually live in Bohemia.

Still, there was something all too perfect about the fairy-tale city around me. Two saints with freshly painted halos that looked like helicopter blades stared at me from atop the Charles Bridge. They were, I supposed, the first NATO-ready Czechs. Below them, English-speaking buskers strummed Dylan tunes on battered guitars. Michael Kaufman, who edits a local journal, may have put his finger on it when he said, "Prague is a Potemkin Village built by tourist money. The Czech economy is in shambles. They have no money for F-16s."

Be that as it may, you can't get absinthe legally anywhere else, and the je ne sais quoi—how do you say that in Czech?—necessary to inspire an artist, still gushes bountifully from the nymph by the New Town Hall.

A Simple Heart

I n these days of confessional frenzy, voluntary and coerced, every story
is under suspicion. From writers wallowing in the details of affairs with
famous people to witnesses spilling their guts under oath, the land is
awash in hypocrisy. It is therefore, oh, so refreshing, to receive a nine-page
handwritten letter from a housewife named Char Smith in a small town in
West Virginia.

In 1989 Mrs. Smith, touched by the plight of Eastern Europeans emerging from decades of authoritarian rule, was moved to help a Romanian family. By no means rich, Mrs. Smith was able to contact and visit a family in
the town of Piatra Neamt, and strike a friendship that has endured for ten
years. During these ten years, she has seen a tremendous struggle to survive
as living conditions for these people worsened. "It's almost ten years since
the revolution," she writes, "and look where they are now. I've tried to give
this family hope . . . but though they appreciate my support, my words aren't
meaning as much anymore."

Mrs. Smith writes movingly of the details of this family's life, their fight
to insure an operation for their adopted daughter, their loss of faith in the
future. She rails against the indifference of the Western world after the Cold
War and berates our media for telling us next to nothing about the suffering
of real people. But her own despair lives most tellingly in that simple asser-

tion of fact: "my words aren't meaning as much anymore." Here is the entire relationship of our overaffluent West to the quickly dimming world behind the former Iron Curtain. Our words, whether the words of free-market ideologues, democracy preachers, consumer visionaries, or simple, good-hearted people, do not mean much anymore. Romanians have heard them all, and things are getting bleaker. They have McDonald's and Coca Cola and the rare sympathy of a few pure souls like Mrs. Smith, but their survival is precarious. The magical West brought many things but not a quick way out of the past.

As the IMF licks its wounds over the loss of billions to ex-KGB thieves, and NATO re-creates the Hapsburg Empire, you have to wonder what's in store for Mrs. Smith's friends. Left outside the *nouveau* NATO-Hapsburg Catholic world, they seem relegated to a life understood only instinctively and compassionately by a good soul like the very rare Mrs. Smith. Is that how all stories end?

I kept cringing, as I read the handwritten, crowded, nine-page letter, that something truly awful might come from this story of unselfish friendship. I kept waiting for the other shoe to drop, for something terrible and scandalous to be revealed. But there wasn't. There was only love for a family far away and the despair of living in a world that doesn't care. And that was the most awful thing of all—without a punch line, without a dramatic denouement.

How We Got to Kosovo

I n communist Romania in the 1950s, my classmates were multi-ethnic
and spoke a variety of languages. In my class we had Romanians, Germans, Hungarians, Serbs, Jews, Gypsys, Szekelys, Bulgarians, and
Greeks. We spoke a hodgepodge of languages and got along fine because it
was forbidden by the government to speak ill of people's nationalities or ori-
gins. Our parents were too afraid, at least during Stalinism, to tell us the
horrible history that had brought all these different people together. They
didn't tell us about all the fighting, over hundreds of years, over the same
piece of real estate, or about the slights and insults, real or imagined,
recorded in the collective memory and kept alive by hundreds of small
sayings, sentimental songs, drunken ditties, morbid fairy tales, and musty
chronicles.

Without knowing it at the time, I had the misfortune of belonging to one
of the top-hated categories. I was Jewish, from a Hungarian and Polish background, and my mother, who was Jewish, had remarried a Romanian from a
part of the country hated by everyone, including the local Romanians. I
didn't know that my hometown had been the subject of territorial disputes
between the Austro-Hungarian and the Ottoman empires, then between
the nations of Romania and Hungary. These facts were relayed to us in a
highly comforting version in history class, a version that blamed all misfor-

tune on class relations and tensions within economic systems. And was this version wrong? Not necessarily. The problem with it is that it left out the one unpredictable element that usually renders nonsensical the best theories, namely, people's deep-seated and emotionally unassailable stupidity.

This stupidity, which is one of the great unanalyzed factors in all history, not just that of the Balkans, is composed of the belief that the stink of one's family and tribe is vastly superior to the familial stink of the neighboring tribe; that your language is wittier or deeper; that the sounds you make when you wail away about your love for the muddy ravine in which you were conceived is much, much more melodic than the wailing of your neighbors; that the smoke-darkened icons cut out of old magazines that hang on your wall are true representations of the only gods worth praying to, and that the gods and prayer habits of the people over the hill are unspeakable offenses that will cease only when you have killed them. This kind of stupidity is like a sturdy weed: you can weed several times a day and, in the morning, there it is again.

In 1989 the official narcotic ideology that went by the name "socialism" was officially kaput, but the people who had been in charge were not kaput at all. Their way to hold on to power was to remind people of the undying hatred they once felt for their neighbors. Suddenly, all those sentimental songs and nasty ditties recording all the slights suffered throughout history at the hands of people with whom they had gotten along just fine for about forty years, bubbled up and started intoxicating everybody with the bittersweet juice of eternal victimization.

Among the mobsters who percolated out of the communist apparatchik muck after 1989, Milosevic of Yugoslavia is the worst. He stripped his country and his people of all the three conditions necessary for the eradication of historic stupidity: peace, a good economy, and good leadership.

This is all the more tragic since Yugoslavia, even while still part of the great socialist camp, had already made more economic progress than all its other Balkan neighbors. We, in Romania, looked with envy at the standard of living of Yugoslav workers and to their freedom to travel and to bring money back home to build private homes and start small businesses. And, indeed, you have to go no further than the Olympic Games in Sarajevo to see a prosperous, Western-style city, in which young people in blue jeans listened to rock 'n' roll on their Sony Walkmans and filled up the coffeehouses and bars, flirting and talking across ethnic lines, without any self-consciousness. Today, the beautiful city of Sarajevo is in ruins, more than half its people dead or in exile, its fine historical buildings piles of rubble—all of it courtesy of Milosevic, the man who today cries foul because his murdering thugs are being checked by NATO bombs.

Exiles, All

For my literary generation, exile had only one direction: France. When my mother and I made the momentous decision to leave our homeland forever, my interests and hers differed. I looked forward to being in the company of Tristan Tzara, E. M. Cioran, Paul Celan, and Eugen Ionesco, the great French-bound exiles of previous generations. My mother, on the other hand, looked to the bourgeois comfort of America. I despised her for this utilitarianism and vowed to conquer France as soon as I could get away from my mother's America, which she imposed on me by the sheer force of her seniority and economic clout.

The romantic myth of exile was possible in its full, unexamined glory only in the mind of an adolescent in the mid-sixties of our century. At that time, alienation was philosophically fashionable, even necessary, and exile had become the crème of alienation, the acme of youthful despair. We maintained the generation gap with all the assiduity of housemaids. Every removal from home, from my very real exile to a precollege Grand Tour of Europe on a shoestring, was gravely experienced by my contemporaries as existential estrangement (in different concentrations, of course; the metaphorical containing, usually, only 10 percent of the potency of the real thing).

The reality of exile, visible in a realistic light several decades later, had in fact been very different for my predecessors. Far from a celebration of estrangement, it had been heartbreaking. For Cioran, the author of *Un précis de décomposition*, his condition was a prompt to suicide. Paul Celan, whose parents were murdered by the Nazis, saw his continued existence as a mistake and committed suicide, finally, in Paris. Ionesco, who had taken Europe by storm by pointing a mirror at its absurd manners, was situated at the intersections of two totalitarianisms, a position that was hardly playful. Tristan Tzara, who had founded the Dada provocation, became a communist, which was a form of artistic suicide very much like a real one. The list of literal and metaphorical suicides of Romanian exiles is long, and the same is true for exiles from every other country who had the misfortune of being born in one of the century's dark decades.

Part Four

The Devil's Art:

Autobiography

Adding Life, Erasing the Record

1.

I am going to address two forms of life-telling: the automatic and the palliative. The first was once, but is no longer, vulnerable to social revolution, the second is a perennial placebo, and the subject of this essay.

Let's start with the first: Is it possible to have a life without having a biography?

On the face of it, the answer would be yes, but on further thought I'd say that, yes, before the advent of the modern, bureaucratic state it was possible. The bureaucratic state, however, inscribed every individual with the infrastructure of biography. You can even say that the state invented the individual by means of biography. The individual is someone with a recorded birth, marriage, school attendance, property deeds, employment record, and death certificate. The individual is the writing that defines him. It is not possible to be an individual without a biography. It is illegal to be an individual without a biography. The state sees to it—through the recorded infrastructure—that each individual has a unique biography. The official infrastructure is filled out over a lifetime by the modern individual with a network of paper trails: correspondence, inter-office memos, faxes, e-mail, tape and video recordings. There is little difficulty in biographing anyone alive after the mid-eighteenth century in Europe or North America, and what little difficulty there is has to do with the overabundance of data and the need to select. The biographical act of the state is automatic and increasingly weighty while the biographical subject is increasingly baroque and circumscribed.

The radical act under such circumstances is to erase or overthrow the record, either in favor of tabula rasa—through revolution—or by writing one's autobiography. I'm using *revolution* here to mean anarchy, i.e, the moment of the burning of the Office of the Registrar and the Archive of the Secret Police, but it's just a symbolic trope. Such "revolution" is no longer possible since our biographies are no longer centralized but spread farther than most individuals travel, with bits and pieces lodged and multiplied in databases that are everywhere and nowhere at once.

We moderns, or postmoderns, are overwritten. Overinscribed. Overrecorded. The modern state is an automatic overproducer of individual biographies. The necessity to control every aspect of human existence, down to and beyond the molecular level, is an automatic function of the bureaucratic machine. The overabundance of biography is also a result of democracy. In theocratic societies only kings and nobles had biographies. Subjects were known only by their functions: butlers, weavers, blacksmiths, buttressers, picklers, seamstresses, moat diggers. The nameless serf layers below the professionals were known only as "souls."

Souls don't have biographies, they have only a collective life and, if they are good, a private afterlife. The modern state and increasing democracy gave these souls back their bodies, unique bodies with the marks of identity on them. The body is the biography. It is the body, gained through social revolutions in the eighteenth and ninteenth centuries, that provides the records of the state and is now overproducing enough data to create not just the individual to whom it belongs but other bodies as well, whether fictional or cloned.

The only way to subvert one's official biography is to rewrite it. Autobiography is the opposite of the biography insofar as it is the individual's attempt to escape the description of the state. Some autobiographers might deny this, pointing to their use of official records, etc., but in effect, their texts exist for the purpose of challenging those records. When one begins a tale with the words "I was born in Pontoise in 1456," one will spend the rest of one's argument, indifferent of whether one was born in Pontoise or not, on decrying or apologizing for that fact. The misfortune of being born—to paraphrase Cioran—along with all the other misfortunes deemed fit for the record, is what autobiographers target for destruction. Every autobiography is an antisocial, subversive act aimed against the recorded facts of one's life.

Autobiography subverts the data-heavy body by attempting to give back the individual his soul, to return the body-specifics to the collective matrix. Autobiographers aspire to be serfs of undifferentiated energy. Autobiography subverts not only the state but the body, which is the biography authored by the state. The autobiographer makes a claim to immortality. The body is, of course, mortal, and the state, while it encourages reproduction, is fond of occasional house-cleaning.

And now along comes virtuality, which empties the body and makes possible the overwriting of the soul. To give just one example: the Paper Body of the President has grown so vast in half a century it is quite impossible to see. The librarian of Jimmy Carter's presidential library in Atlanta told me that Roosevelt, who was a four-term president and oversaw some of the most dramatic events of our century—the Great Depression, World War II—had less than half as many papers as Carter, a one-term president. The librarian dreaded to imagine the size of Clinton's White House archive where every e-mail is backed by a hard copy and every copy is copied. When such dimensions are reached, the body becomes invisible. Proportion dictates that monuments cannot rise above a certain height without disappearing. The Body of the Nation, following closely on the Body of the President, is likewise drowning or dissolving in biographical overabundance.

Just in time, virtuality and unlimited memory rushes to our defense. Bill Gates mounted on a chip is to biography and the state what Joan of Arc on her horse was to Orléans and to France: a Savior of the Code, the Guarantor of the infinity of the form. In the virtual world we can rewrite our biography, autobiographomanicize to our heart's content. We can also change identities altogether, slipping out of bodies and genders quicker than it takes to change clothes. We can shape-shift across species, we can spin in the changing rooms of MUDs (multiuser dungeons) as fast as we want. Virtuality has put evolution on fast forward. But this Darwin-on-speed mode is only as good as the data, which is to say that the disembodied soul made possible by the computer is programmed by a writing that is neither less nor more than the abstracted biography of the state. Which is, of course, the abstract of all the biographies of individuals. This tail-swallowing is only seemingly generative of soul. The freedom to muck around in the aesthetics of identity is a game. Virtuality means just that. The textual metarmophosis of the virtual autobiographer is as bound by the fundamental program as the body is to the state.

More tragically, the creation of any fiction of identity is only an admission of the bondage to state, time, and language. What, then, is the state of autobiography in a sea of drifting facts that can fit with ease anywhere, in a world where collage is the predominant mode of expression? And where the image, composed in whatever manner one wishes, remains uniformly contained? Is there an approach that does not require the reinvention of a moral system? Which, given the tattered remains of such systems, adrift across the sands of a psychology in retreat before machines, is, you have to admit, no easy task.

2.

Autobiography! What a bourgeois conceit! What odd presumption that one's life matters enough to write about. One writes autobiography either to escape life or to make some if there isn't enough. In any case, the activity bares the pattern and makes escape—from that point on—difficult unless one writes one autobiography after another, each one in flagrant opposition to the one that came before. Serial lives like (concomitant) sentences.

I have done that—to my embarrassment. My first autobiography, titled modestly, *The Life & Times of an Involuntary Genius*, was written in the third person with a long section—a letter to my first love—in the second. By removing myself, at age 23, from the scant facts of my life, I was hoping to create a listenable story, much the same way that someone calling a help line might say, "I have this friend with a problem." Of course, the reason I wrote an autobiography at such a tender age was that I had the problem of all tender-aged people, namely, I was unknown. By telling this tale of a young man with an exemplary life story I was hoping to remedy that situation. The advantage of writing at such a tender age was that I remembered everything or nearly everything that happened to me. I had the benefit of only a few events, earth-shattering as they might have seemed to me, and I used them to create an initiatory structure. I had no ax to grind but I had (already!) some excuses to make. I left my country and my girl and I felt bad about it. By writing those things down I recast them to appear heroic: I wasn't a traitor, I was an exile, a hero. History came to my aid there, with its long and distinguished list of exile-heroes.

My second autobiography, *In America's Shoes*, picked up where the first one left off, at the beginning of my life in America, and it was a first-person record of the rapid process of becoming American. I felt that by changing countries and languages I had literally been born again. In this sense, I was not starting where I'd left off, but from my new birth in 1966 in Detroit, Michigan. Furthermore, the book is mostly about my life in California, a part of America where the remaking of one's identity was the chief business of the inhabitants. This book is less a record of the past as a writing of the present in its becoming past. The speeded-up nature of time in America is the real subject of this work. In America, I had noticed from the very beginning, the future becomes the past before anyone could possibly understand it. I was hoping to invent a way by which thinking about the past could be made as fast as the transformation itself. The Gogolian sentence, as I understood it from Nabokov's description, with its endless clauses, rolling open parentheses, and constant digressions, was the tool for such enterprise. This book is an autobiography-on-the-run, a "meditation in an emergency," as Frank O'Hara put it. It is also an American book because it made use of the "open field" as theorized by Charles Olson, Robert Duncan, Frank O'Hara, Ted Berrigan, and others, which is to say that it rode the wave of time even as it explained the drowning.

My third autobiography—which was never published—was intended as an autobiography from everyone else's point of view. I mailed out about a hundred questionnaires to friends and acquaintances asking them a number of questions like: "When did we meet? What did we do? What happened afterwards? How do I figure in your life?" I got back a great variety of answers. Some writers took the questions as an opportunity to reminisce scrupulously, others as a license to invent. There were true and fantastic stories in the mix, all of them stylistically incompatible. I realized a number of things: First of all, I was not as important to others as I was to myself. My friends' accounts of our moments together were tawdry and pale compared to how I conceived of them. Second, one's biography from the perspective of others was as loosely connected as subatomic particles: Immense spaces sat between events, attracted only by forces too weak to make a compelling fiction. The biography provided by the state was more substantial than the memories of my friends.

Lately, the autobiographical enterprise has been enjoying great popularity in this country. The imprecise and fuzzy word used to describe this new, hot product is "memoir." I understand the rationale. "Memoir" bypasses even the minimum requirements of the genre as we understood it until now. "Memoir" recognizes the fallibility of memory, the impossibility of ordering what is recalled randomly. What "memoir," like "autobiography," does not relinquish, however, is the right to claim an initiatory structure. These things that happened to me, both forms say, retell an exemplary initiation. The hero leaves home in search of self-fulfillment, encounters many dangers, is transformed into an adult, and returns to slay the dragons of conformity by becoming the head of the household. Or something like that. The endings, in recognition of established postmodern findings, are sometimes open-ended. What is sure is that they do not end in the death of the hero, like novels, because an autobiographer cannot fake his own death. By not dying, the hero of an autobiography always triumphs. The form is implicitly optimistic and as such, American. We do not, in this country, believe in endings: we believe in success. We want to hear stories of triumph. Which is why you will hear only Europeans proclaiming "the death" of this or that, whether "history" or "politics" or "God" or "philosophy" or whatever. We like to think that those things are only metaphors for the "death of Europe." Things in this country do not die, they collapse in a data-subconscious from where they can be retrieved by your zip-drive. The American form of parting with the past is amnesia. We simply forget things by storing them away in our data banks. We have more computer memory in this country than the rest of the world combined. This memory allows us to do computation on a scale impossible before, computations so vast that they allow for the discovery and transformation of everything, including our identities and species. But, as I said before, this is only virtuality. What happens in the bodied world is another story.

What happens in the bodied world is that the collapsed pasts, presents, and futures that we forget as soon as we create them continue a nonvirtual existence in us that gives birth to a great number of monstrous, grotesque, unforeseen fleurs-de-mal, of which "memoirs" are but one product.

What kind of literature is the memoir?

The coincidence factory that is the novel lends its machinery to the manufacture of autobiography—a risk-free loan since there is hardly any wear and tear on the machines. The facts that are made to coincide are preexistent. The novel, on the other hand, is rough on these machines because it forces them to manufacture the facts as well as fit them together.

What machines are there in the coincidence factory?

Perhaps we should first ask what coincidence is. According to Bill Moyers's recovering-addict son, William Cope Moyers, "Coincidence is God's way of remaining anonymous."[*] As my friend Laura says, God *needs* to remain anonymous because if we knew who and where he was we'd kick his ass for some of these coincidences . . . like, let's say, turning eighteen when they give a World War. And furthermore, my friend Kuniko says, there may be many gods and they are all forgetful.

The writer, on the other hand, openly piles coincidence on coincidence in order to create a fate (a book) and advertises his presence at every seam. We know who and where the writer is at all times in a book: He is wherever two unlikely events or characters meet and he is that which puts them together. The postmodern writer has tried to elude this trap by making his presence obvious, by displaying the stage mechanics, a subterfuge intended paradoxically, to obscure his presence. If everything is visible everything is seamless: The Logos is at all times in motion, an ocean, everything is part of it. It is a fine theoretical dodge, but no book can be endless though it can (ideally) be porous. Language itself, all on its own, operates under a set of very strict rules and it displays a terrifyingly cogent machinery, a web that is symmetrical, geometrical, the same in every sound, syllable, word, utterance, story. So who needs to crudely manufacture coincidence when coincidence is inescapable?

We manufacture toys, don't we? It's a process: First we know that the Logos is connected at all points with whatever it passes through. Then we pretend not to know it and call this willful ignorance Mystery, as a palliative against the terror of the real mystery of connection, coincidence, and ineluctability. Then we create our version of a cogent Logos from the artificially willed blind spots where we have disconnected our consciousness. Eureka, we have a novel. We have a story. In the case of an autobiography, the job is a bit harder because we have to ignore not only the tedious cogency of Logos but the facts of our lives such as they are, courtesy of a selective memory. To spin the facts into crude coincidence, fit them into the procrustean bed of the book, takes a will greater than that of the novelist, an ignorance deeper than that of a simple spinner of tales. We who pretend

---

[*]William Cope Moyers, quoted in "Bill Moyers' Son: Good Connections and Bad Addictions," *New York Times*, 20 March 1998.

to tell our lives are the lowest among writers, a tribe not known for its integrity in the first place.

How can a pretender to the job of god have any integrity?

As for the machines themselves, they are the traditional ones of fiction: plot, dialogue, characterization (I almost wrote "cauterization"), exposition, etc. The once-taken-for-granted sobriety of the autobiographer has been pretty much abandoned by the memoirist. Re-created dialogue, falsified plot, impressionistic characterization, and self-serving exposition are pretty much standard—sometimes covered with a thick syrup of lyricality that passes, in some circles, for poetry. Where the circumspect autobiographer of forty years ago might say, "I hear those words from a half century ago as if they were spoken today," and then goes on to make them up, the contemporary memoirist no longer bothers. With this sort of touch there is little, as I've said, wear and tear on the machines of fiction, but what is lost in accuracy is not gained in imagination. Many of today's memoirs, with a few notable exceptions, namely those of scientists and camp survivors, are just fairy tales, primitive novels intended to palliate a public seized by the fear of failure. Failure is un-American. The confessional mania that possesses us today has emptied the nation's closets on television, on radio, in newspapers, in memoirs. Nothing is hidden any longer, but the desire for what is hidden is increased a hundredfold. The open maw of insatiable media need, and the public desire it stimulates and frustrates, demands more and more from the ransacked closets. But fear not: The production of false memory is a booming business. False Memory Syndrome is no longer limited to pop psychologists and their distressed charges, it is the status quo of the moment. The memoir is a skeumorph. Which is to say, a content-empty form anyone can put their stuff in, like Etch-A-Sketch.

Against Synchronicity

We, the people of this earth who are neither rich nor particularly good-looking, like synchronicity. Synchronicity makes us feel important. When synchronicity happens, we believe that the universe has not forgotten us after all. We believe also that synchronicity happens to the rich and photogenic more often than it does to the not-those. Surely, it is only coincidence, fortunate happenstance, and lucky junctions—aspects of synchronicity, that is—that account for wealth and good looks. But a closer look reveals something quite unsettling. Everything is synchronous, there is nothing that doesn't rhyme with something else, no matter how strange or unlikely. Synchronicity rules chaos with an iron hand, and it is only the merciful defense of some kind of brain filter that keeps us from going mad seeing how it all fits together. When this brain defense wears thin, we see the mind-boggling connectiveness of every event in time and space, and reel from the nausea of unrelenting synchronicity.

My brain's defenses were pretty thin the evening I went to a Jungian Elvophile houseboat party at the Lakefront in New Orleans. The Jungians were in town for a conference, and they had gotten together on the houseboat to celebrate their latest addition to the gallery of archetypes: Elvis. It was a blue velvety evening and the breeze off Lake Ponchartrain ruffled fetchingly the Blue Hawaii and other Elvine-costuming of the guests. Of all the professionals who gather for boat parties anywhere in the world, the Jungians are the greatest believers in synchronicity. They achieve this belief through the study of dreams and the application upon these dreams of a gridded array of frozen timeless figures called archetypes. Anyway, I asked a Jungian analyst where she was from, and she said, "San Francisco." "Funny," I said, "I'm going to San Francisco tomorrow to speak at the San Francisco State University about baseball." "No, you're not," she said, "You're going to the University of San Francisco to speak about baseball, and I am the boss of the man who hired you to speak." We both agreed that this was synchronicity indeed, come to the help of my confused mind. Moments later, an architecture professor made a comment about museums that resembled exactly something I'd written that day. A few moments after that, a Republican pathologist bemoaned the hijack of the Republican party by the Christian right, which had been the exact subject of an earlier conversation with a Methodist minister who had recalled for me a dream I had had exactly two weeks before. As the evening progressed, synchronicity became so palpable you could touch it. The cardboard cutout of Elvis watched over all this from behind the piano. The Elvis lookalike bartender with the pasted-on sideburns poured whiskey in thick déjà-vu glasses the likes of which I have at home.

There were other instances of synchronicity that lasted into the night. I am only recalling this to warn everyone: Stay away from noticing too many connections in the real world. They lead to riches and good looks for some, but the vast majority simply goes mad.

While writing this I heard a mockingbird in the magnolia outside the window making typing sounds identical to mine.

Collecting

I was strolling with the novelist Robert Olen Butler on Royal Street looking in antique shop windows when Butler leaned close and whispered: "Do you collect anything?" There was something shocking about the way he said it, almost as if he were asking me to reveal something sexually intimate. It reminded me of a coworker at the 8th Street Bookstore in New York who asked me years ago in a whisper: "Are you Athenian?," which I couldn't, for the longest time, figure out. Until one day I asked him, "What's an Athenian?" "Queer," he said. Oh.

Anyway, Butler is a collector of the illustrated cards that used to come inside cigarette packages early in the century. He may collect other things, too, but I didn't ask. The subject of collecting makes me feel awkward and guilty. I have always been prey to a conflict between collecting things and getting rid of them. When I was a kid I was very taken with my stamp collection. Then one day I got in a fight with my stepfather, and the bastard sold my stamps. At age thirteen I started reading and collecting poetry books. I had a glass case full of books by poets and I dusted and alphabetized them every week until I got so many the case overflowed and I had to stack them on top of everything else, including my school desk. When my room, which was more like a closet, filled up with books by Romanian poets, I started doing my homework in the kitchen. The stepfather was gone by then, but the books got sold anyway because we left the country forever. Back then, when you left a country, you left it forever.

Collectors are possessed by a kind of creative pride. A collection is like a novel, it tells the story of a certain attention, exercised over time. Things have very little intrinsic value. They have to be plucked out of the great sea of objects out there and made to shine by their election, and then they have to be loved to yield any kind of pleasure. Not to mention dusted. I don't think that many collectors actually contemplate their objects a great deal. The rush of having them, adding to them, and knowing that one is the creator of the story they tell is quite sufficient. I know that I didn't read many of the books I owned. Reading them messed up their perfect jackets, cracked their snappy spines. There is something innocent and childlike about collecting, an imaginative sweetness made of greed, curiosity, and the desire to be Linnaeus. There is also something sexual and criminal about it, a kind of pervert thrill that will make you do anything to get the stuff you need, which explains Butler's furtiveness.

Grave robbing is the world's second oldest profession. The pyramids were looted as soon as the overseers left the area. The Spanish robbed all the graves of meso-America. Ancient Greece is in the British Museum. There are countless collectors in America. At one point, early in the twentieth century, rich American tourists almost collected all of Europe and Latin America. I guess that if you don't have a long history you can always collect one. What good is being rich if you don't have a family history? Or, conversely, what good is being poor even if you descend from Charlemagne?

The end of my collections came about because of circumstances. Moving around hasn't made it easy to keep things. "Every move is like a fire," say the people from U-Haul, and they should know. Still, I was greatly relieved each time, even as I indulged in a certain regret. Having no things means freedom. Most people are held hostage by their stuff, even just junk. Most things collect by themselves, without much creative will behind them. If a random accretion of objects can make one stationary, imagine what a collection can do. It can pin you to the wall of your abode like a butterfly in a lepidopterium.

I have always prized freedom over everything else, but now and then I sigh.

The Strangeness of Languages

I had five years of Russian in high school and not a word of it stuck to me. For years I blamed it on my Russian teacher, Comrade Papadapolou, who wore the first miniskirt in Eastern Europe and prevented me from concentrating properly. Later I blamed the politics: No self-respecting Romanian should learn the language of the oppressor. But years have passed and now I have a new theory. I was in the Czech Republic for a month and not a word of that Slavic language stuck to me long enough to make use of it. Not even *dak-oui* (thank you) or *prosim* (please), which everyone says. The reason, I now believe, is that there are certain sounds that are unnatural to my brain or at least find the passages blocked. Give me any Latin-based language and I'll be holding forth with the natives on the subtler aspects of garlic usage. But the Slavic meets a shiny, mirrorlike surface that sends the words right back. Linguists say that everybody has receptors for all the languages because all of them are derived from an Ur-language that was broken up by God in Babylon because we chattered too much about irrelevant matters. Babylonian chatter has multiplied since then a few billion times, especially since the advent of cellular phones, but that's another story.

The reason *my* receptors for Slavic are missing is that my ancestors had lived in these parts and were being constantly attacked by people speaking Slav dialects. One Cossack too many shut down something in the universal receptor. The other thing, of course, is that different languages issue from different parts of the body. English comes from the middle of the chest, French from the throat, Italian from the cheeks, and Slav languages from the belly. For the One-Cossack-Too-Many reason, I cannot speak from my belly, which is the chief concern of people who like to drink a lot of beer. The Czech Republic leads the world in beer consumption. Because I cannot speak from my belly and my receptors are blocked, I have to regretfully conclude that I'll never be able to contact the natives. I even tried speaking in tongues by making lots of *shshsh* sounds, but it came out sounding like pidgin Latin. Damn history will never leave you alone, even if all you want to do is say, "Hi, it's a beautiful day. Do you have any food without bread dumplings?" Babylon was a disaster, and I pay the price.

Animals: The Thin Furry Line Between
Us and the Devil

I've heard it said, all too often, that human beings differ from animals by their ability to laugh. This, like most things repeated more than three times, isn't true. I see animals laughing all the time. Their merriment spans the range from the smile of the Cheshire cat to the foolish grin of this horse I once caught looking at my date when we went out for a "walk in the country."

More to the point, one should ask what the animals are laughing at. The answer, I'm sorry to say, is: they are laughing at us. Since most animals don't speak human (some of them do but prefer not to) they have delegated humorists to articulate what exactly they are laughing at. I am one of those delegated by the animals to speak, so I'll get to it right away.

Animals laugh at humans, but not all animals laugh at the same humans and not at the same things even when they do. Some humans are hard to laugh at, and only predatory cats like the leopard are able to laugh at such humans as the chairman of the Federal Reserve, for instance. Animals also find it hard to laugh at humorists per se and are most seriously attentive when one is speaking on their behalf. Still, a few general *raisons-de-rire* are common among animals, and I will list them in order of animal importance:

First, humans use money. This is the source of much merriment among vertebrates and invertebrates alike. They are amused by our constantly trying to find money to get what we need and then to find more money to get what we don't need. It really breaks them up to see us surrounded by junk we can't eat. Animals get what they need without any money and they eat it all on the spot. Some animals laugh only halfheartedly at this human folly, however, because they realize that our pursuit threatens their existence directly. Humans have destroyed the animals' homes and they eat the animals, too. Most animals stop laughing while they are being cooked, but some animals, such as the lowly chicken and the pig, are known to laugh in our mouth *while they are being eaten*. This, I know, is hard to believe, and I can only explain it by dint of the fact that the animal sense of humor tends to be generous and self-effacing.

Second, animals laugh at our mating habits. To them, we look ridiculous scurrying to charm one another with inedible things (most animals consider chocolates inedible) and then, after we conquer each other, sneaking out and conquering others behind the backs of our first conquests. They are mightily tickled too by all the elaborate care we take in our mating rituals and the ridiculous positions some of us assume when performing the physics of coupling. Animals giggle incontrollably when they see people spraying their bodies with flower stinks and consulting books on how to please their partners. Many animals like to roll in flowers, too, but they certainly don't stop to read books about mating.

Third, wearing furs that come off and don't belong to us in any case. This again, is occasion only for halfhearted amusement because it's hard to laugh while bleeding to death after your pelt has been ripped from your body. There have been animals who advocated revenge for this sort of thing, but lack of money and weaponry has so far prevented effective action. So they laugh instead.

Fourth, wearing clothes, in general.

Fifth, our biological ignorance. No animals, no matter how weird their behaviors, ever keep themselves ignorant of their own death. They know it's going to happen. Watching people strutting about as if there was no tomorrow makes beasts laugh, but, once again, it worries some of them because this attitude leads many human beings to mistreat animals as well as their own kind. Creatures who think themselves immortal get easily bored. In order to alleviate their boredom they seek better and stronger entertainments and, quite often, they get pleasure from the suffering of others. This worrisome tendency toward cruelty keeps some animals from laughing at all.

Some of them remember as far back as the Roman Colosseum and are not pleased at all.

Sixth, animals crack up when they see humans imagining themselves living after death in all kinds of perfect places that resemble luxury hotels, or, on the contrary, roasting forever in fires of pitch and guilt. Animals watch people go into big, empty buildings called churches and talk to themselves in there, until they are so impressed with themselves that they try to convince others to come to their building. When others refuse to follow them, they sometimes kill them.

Not all animals are convinced that people should know that they are being laughed at about this. Some of them cautioned me against mentioning anything about this matter, but I reassured them that a humorist named Mark Twain, among many others, had already carried this message to humans. This Twain, you see, was speaking mostly for his cat, but he also represented frogs and mules part of the time.

Seventh, animals are amused but not very much by the reasons humans have for killing each other. Humans rarely fight over territory or mates but go to great lengths to extinguish each other over matters of words and habits. People who get along reasonably well for a long time discover suddenly that they are consuming different cheeses and like to sing different songs. For this reason, they attack each other and fight unto death. Animals like to fight over cheese, too, but only if there isn't enough.

These are only a few of the reasons why animals have a hoot over us. In the book-length version of this brief essay, I enumerate all the five hundred reasons and provide the reader with a complete scale of animal laughter as well. Animal laughter spans the range from Subtle-Smirking-with-Whisker-Twitch to Rolling-Wildly-with-Exposed-Belly-Down-Steep-Hillside. Personally, I think that this last type of merriment is exaggerated. We are not *that* funny.

Walking Bear

A 350-pound black bear named No Neck walked all the way from the Florida Panhandle across Alabama, Mississippi, and Louisiana until he got to Baton Rouge. That's the longest walk any recorded bear ever took, and he would have kept walking on to the Atchafalaya Basin where about three hundred black bears live. No Neck was apparently looking for a mate, and the word must have been out among Florida bears that the Atchafalaya Basin community had possibilities. There are so few bears left, they must sense each other in the empty air: The bear frequency must ring with the poignant signals of their dying. No Neck himself had been living in relative contentment in the Apalachicola National Forest until he was caught raiding beehives, arrested, and moved to the Eglin Air Force Base. Now why would anyone arrest a bear for eating honey? That's like arresting a bird for flying. So No Neck, finding himself under arrest, lonely, and distressed by the silence on the once-crowded bear frequency, decided to take off for the Atchafalaya. He walked past shopping malls, where there were once forests, he walked through suburbs where once there were bears, he passed by houses, highways, McDonald'ses, gas stations, and TV towers. He was spotted along the way by people amazed to see him walking like that. He stopped for nothing, accepted no rides, and kept on going. If he had any doubts about his purpose or his eventual destination, we will never

Small devils wear horns of garlic and, as they grow older, they learn to love food and drama. In *Still Life with Mozzarella*, the immortal garlic performs in a Garlic Farce.

(Amy Weiskopf)

Botero's devil, glowing with tenderness, revels in the glories of the flesh right over our housetops, which, magically bewitched, have turned into slices of cheesecake.

(Fernando Botero, *Devil and Woman*. Art Resource, NY)

Actors in a sexual drama involving a complex and amused Cabala—the oranges of Jerusalem meet the swamp actors of New Orleans.
(Amy Weiskopf, *Merlitans and Satsumi*)

The skull authorized any debauches, whether intellectual or carnal, because it was a reminder of the transitory nature of life. Drinking from a skull was *de rigueur* for bonvivants, and using skulls for candleholders was a cliché of student life that persists to this day. The Devil is fond of tradition.
(Amy Weiskopf, *Vanitas with Skull*)

Poor St. Anthony! Swollen from his hallucinations like a madman from drugs, he must suffer the full repertoire of the pagan monsters that once walked the earth in freedom, but which are now mere tools of the Christian Devil.

(Matthias Gruenewald, *The Temptation of St. Anthony*. Erich Lessing/Art Resource, NY)

The Devil wears glasses to better study God's creation in order to enslave and destroy it. Children, beware: excessive reading, excessive study, excessive curiosity, and excessive gazing lead to excessive interiority, which leads downward to Hell, not upward to the simplicity of Heaven. In Cambodia, people wearing glasses were killed because they were suspected of being teachers, polyglots, and readers or, in the eyes of the Khmer Rouge, Devils.

(Joseph Thaddaeus Stammel, *A Devil Wearing Eyeglasses*. Erich Lessing /Art Resource, NY)

The poet sleeps because he has put in a full nightshift of delighted and wicked work. In the light of day, he is saved from the wrath of Judgment only by the loving brush of his mate.

(Alice Henderson, *Poet Sleeping*)

The Devil's favorite bar in New Orleans has hours as rich as those of the Duc de Berry. Working the night shift here, the author has accumulated a number of indulgences good for the better sections of Hell (see Fra Angelico).

(Kerri McCaffety, Two interior shots of Molly's)

The Duc de Berry, who commissioned the Very Rich Hours to entertain his jaded senses, was particularly fond of the Imagination. The Devil is gratified here by both his earthly senses and his boundless Imagination that redeems the tormented after thoroughly enjoying them. The Voyeur extracts Salvation by pulling the Spirit out of the Flesh like a mollusk from a shell.

(Jean Colombe, *Hell*, from the *Tres Riches Heures du Duc de Berry*. Giraudon/Art Resource, NY)

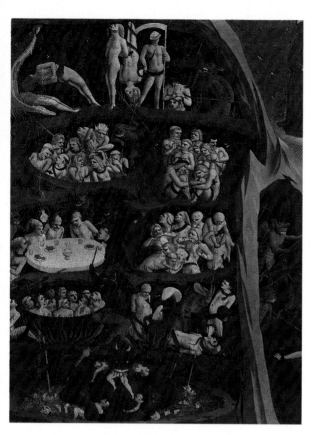

In this special section of Hell, which is the Devil's favorite, the damned are exquisite and tortured exquisitely. One can only imagine, with some frissons, the audition.
(Fra Angelico, *The Last Judgment*. Erich Lessing /Art Resource, NY)

(below)
Here is the Devil as Pan and Godfather, old god of nature, dispensing pleasure and power to lust-driven witches, and blessings on his spawn. There is a certain panic behind his eyes, as if he hears the footsteps of the Inquisition in the distance.
(Francisco Goya, *Witches' Sabbath*. Erich Lessing/Art Resource, NY)

Catholic tombstones are waiting rooms for the Day of Judgment. In their little perennial houses, the dead rehearse their defense for the Almighty, and rest for the day when they will be called to rise and utilize their creaky bodies again.

(Sandra Russell Clark, *Greenwood,* from *Elysium: A Gathering of Souls: New Orleans Cemeteries*) know. The wildllife authorities tracking him were ready to help him cross Highway 55, but in the end they decided to bring him down near Baton Rouge. They shot him with a tranquilizer dart and took him back to the Apalachicola National Forest where he'd been arrested in the first place. He might have been allowed to make it to the black bear community in Atchafalaya, but it was feared that the heavily industrial and populated shore of the Mississippi would bring him in conflict with rifle-toting humans. No Neck knew where he was going but so did we: his ear was tagged, his lip tattooed, and he had an electronic collar. Back in his forest, No Neck may be too dispirited to raid hives. He probably doesn't care that he set a bear-walking record. He's still lonely, and at night he dreams of strange towering shapes that broadcast to humans in frequencies he cannot and doesn't care to access. But that's how we heard his story and that's all that we will ever know. His bear frequency is inaccessible to us.

Grandfatherhood

Well, I'm a grandfather. What of it? Grandbébé Marcus is three months old and when I hold him I feel ancient, like a tree. I hold his light, light person, weighing about the same as an average grocery bag, and feel this awesome shoot of energy. His eyes light and widen when he sees me and he smiles, and I am filled with his innocence. Almost everything he sees is for the first time: His gaze finds the things of this world one by one and bathes them in a wide surprised wonder. A bird. A fence. The word *waffle* on the side of the Waffle House. Or perhaps only part of the bird, the red part, and one slat of fence, and the *a* in the waffle. I'm not sure how much of the thing he sees but that much of it lightens up, as if seen for the first time. I can only intuit, like a man in the dark, the vastness of that first gaze.

His innocence makes me feel simultaneously guilty and awed; guilty because I have forgotten how it was to look on something for the first time; I have even forgotten how to look on something *as if it were* the first time. That's the essence of grandfatherhood then: to have twice forgotten innocence, in both its primary mystery and in the awareness of its necessity. That is what grandbébé Marcus teaches, in his Osh Kosh farmer overalls bulging over diaper, and plump feet like two white yams. My son tells me that one whole month before Marcus laughed while awake, he laughed in his sleep.

What did he laugh at in his dreams, way before he found something to laugh at in our world? Did things present themselves to him in their hilarious wholeness before he actually saw them? I feel him struggling with his body as its needs assert themselves and his laughter changes to crying: hunger, gas, discomfort, growing muscles, tingling nerves, excess of light, heat, cold, all the facts of the body surging through fields of discovery outside himself. Or maybe there is no *outside himself* yet, only a plane of sensations intersecting each other at speeds inconceivable to the slow, diminishing, dim grandfather-tree holding him between two huge limbs. The work of generations, the measure of time—they weigh about twenty pounds, have eyes that widen in astonished delight, their name is Marcus, who invents the world as he finds it.

Love in the Nineties

My friend William Talcott, a poet and a gentleman, complains most bitterly about love in the nineties. He offers himself as an example. He'd fallen madly in love with an unhappily married Japanese woman who reciprocated this love, but then returned to her husband, a boring guy who threatened to drown himself if she didn't rejoin the fold. In response, William produced a beautiful book of verse, entitled *Benita's Book,* which was his lover's name. Like all poets, he credits his beloved with magical powers: "You're also in / my thoughts Benita, your power to heal / imaginary ailments just by smiling." Of course, it would seem from this that the poet knows that his ailments are imaginary, but you don't know poets. Here is what he says next: "When we touch / that place moves where all lovers go— / a pasture by the sea / and you can ride the ponies there." No longer ailing, he now transports Benita to that imaginary, though crowded, place where lovers and ponies surf. Now, it's easy to find the brokenhearted pathetic, but consider the alternative. "The other day," William writes to me, "I was on the trolley eavesdropping on two animated young men, discussing the merits of Levi's 505s versus 512s." Enough said. The callousness in the body proper is clearly but a reflection of the callousness in the body politic.

Another poet, friend of mine, Jim Nisbet, has also produced a wrenching volumette of the heart entitled *Across the Tasman Sea*. It is the story of a poet abandoned by a woman who chose a professional career over his lyric ministrations. The denouement could have been predicted, since the affair unfolds from letting her drive his car to long-distance phone calls and then, finally, to e-mail. The distance grows as we reach the outer limits of technology, after which the lovers dissolve and the so-called real world reasserts itself. It leaves a poet, Mr. Nisbet in this case, declaring: "Tell me / you're / there / at the end / of this fabulous / bus ride." He knows she won't, but what's imagination for?

The Blessed Waters of Sleep

These days, I dream of sleep. Sweet narcotic of healing, come to me, I beseech, as I toss restlessly amid the real and imaginary reefs of middle-age anxiety. Come to me with all your cool salves, your chasms, your phantoms, and even your hells! I lie awake, reviewing my life, cursing my doctors, disemboweling my enemies, reinterpreting the once sweetly simple, climbing the ladder of the never-ending list of things to do that will never be done. I think of E. M. Cioran, the great philosopher, who suffered also from insomnia: "And while a world interior to our waking solicits us, we envy the indifference, the perfect apoplexy of the mineral," he said. I have tried melatonin, sleeping pills, valerian extract—all in vain. I have even tried to buy the sleep of others, convinced that those who sleep more than their share are possessed of a magical substance. As I think of the sleepers, the gifted ones, the young, the unconcerned, sleep recedes even further. It isn't fair: I, who am a worshipper of dreams, am locked out of the kingdom of dreams, while others, who have neither the vision nor the skill to fully tend their dreams, get to roll like pigs in the treasures of the moon goddess.

It was not always thus. I was a sleepy child once in a dreamy city in a slumbering country at the edge of Europe. Romania was steeped in the sleep of centuries, from which history woke it loudly every three decades or so, in order to plunge it into a nightmare of death and destruction. My hometown, Sibiu, in Transylvania, was swathed in layered, thick walls, still sporting moss-covered cannonballs from the countless sieges it endured. Inside these walls we slept, my fellow burghers and I, while the half-lidded, somnolent eyes of attics in the steep roofs, watched over our nights. All of our houses, built in the thirteenth century, had owls. They perched on trunks full of German encyclopedias, top hats, discarded armor, rolled-up maps. The Pied Piper of Hamelin, it was said, piped the children of Germany over the mountain here, to Sibiu, where they slept.

My kingdom of childhood sleep was vast. I slept in hollows on the dark side of the Teutsch cathedral, I slept on the grass in front of the Astra library, and I slept in school with my head on the books, absorbing more of their wisdom than otherwise possible. My favorite book (not a school book) was A Connecticut Yankee at King Arthur's Court, by Mark Twain. I identified with the Yankee who falls asleep and wakes up in another day and age where his superior knowledge enables him to control the world. I was certain that just over the threshold of my own sleep lay the world meant for me.

Our great romantic poet, Eminescu, spun his verses from moon dust and star gossamer. He dreamed tales of stars who fell in love with mortal girls. Spirits, goblins, ghosts and old sages populated his verse, freshly arrived from the shores of Morphia, goddess of sleep. His poetry fed from the dark soil of fairy tales and songs sung in high mountains beneath sheer walls of granite. The thick forests teemed with creatures eager to enter our dreams: most of them did so directly, but some reached us via Eminescu's poetry. Over in England, Keats, Shelley, Byron, and Coleridge broke open the outer shell of reality's hard nut and let the sweet contents pour out like a purple fog, bringer of dreams, portents, nocturnal voyages. And over in America, Edgar Allan Poe, suspended like a question mark of smoke from the end of his opium pipe, warned the nation of daytime and optimism that a dark dream, an unseen shroud, stretched just below its sunnyness.

The world of sleep is vaster than the world of awakeness. Think of all the nights that stretch from our frightened, monster-haunted human beginnings to the loudness of today when we are doing all we can to banish night. We began in the shelter of the cave, steeped in a nameless dream that had at its center a single flame whose mystery we have not yet fathomed. What was it that woke us from the essential sleep of beasts to the odd knowledge that now compelled us to consider our existence? We awoke from this meditation-dream only when hunger propelled us to kill, and that was good, because for those few hours we forgot the tormenting flame and happily became beasts again. Eating well caused insomnia, however, so we invented song, art, and poetry, to while away the dark. The nights of the neolithic were long.

Humans have slept fitfully since then. At certain times, history seemed to disappear. A pall of sleep settled over certain ages, obscuring the dailiness of what was, after all, no progress, no development, no awakeness. But when history awoke, it did so with huge explosions, with booms, with cannons, with bombs, with bombast, with men on horses and tanks, an unbearable din of boastful assertion, a rejection of sleep. War woke us up from the eternal contemplation of the dream-flame and put us on the path of Insomnia. Our cities are brightly lit odes to Insomnia, our modern economies are the fruits of sleeplessness. Bowed before blinding small screens, the drones of the working world keep on working past their duty, past what is strictly necessary to bring home the food. The evil goddess of Insomnia rules our world as fiercely as sweet sleep once did it.

Who are the partisans of sleep today? Artists, certainly. Dream is our material, the stuff from which we draw art. One can draw wiggly lines of light from us back to the cave painters at Lascaux and see the dreams we dreamt. Some, like Goya, Bosch, Hoffman, Baudelaire, Lautreamont, Rimbaud, Freud, André Breton, declared the poetry of the dream openly. Others simply fed at the dark fountain and felt themselves expand. Some mystical poets have denied the waking world any reality at all, maintaining that we are all a dream in the mind of God, dreaming of that which dreams us. That "that" was once a butterfly for Lao Tsu. Of course, most people of the world have known, just like Lope de Vega, that "la vida es sueño." Even our superficial pop singers give it to us without respite, "life is but a dream, ah, ah!"

Some philosophers and scientists have to be included among artists. Insights bombarded them in sleep, apples hit them with force and revelation, atoms arranged themselves behind their closed eyelids. All thinkers speak with wonder of the state just before sleep, the antechamber of sleep, the residence of Sister Hypnagogia. It is there that most great revelations are encountered. But only those with the fortitude to rise and commit their visions to paper can wrench these jewels from the night.

Pregnant women cherish their sleep, whose calming waters they float in just like the child floats inside them. The amniotic waters of sleep, our first, are also the sites of our first dreams. Today's doctors are as keen on sleep as the early medicine men: They don't know how or why but literal sleep heals it. Whether we are all asleep or not, the vastness of the unconscious is greater than the shards of what we know.

Professional Hazards

D r. Felix Post has some unhappy news. He shouldn't, though, with a name like that. With a name like that he should be a delivery service for happy news. Honey, guess what just came by felix post? Be that as it may, the inaptly named psychiatrist has studied one hundred writers and reported in the *British Journal of Psychiatry* that the profession is a hotbed of mental illness. Poets, he discovered, had more mood swings and manic depression requiring hospitalization than novelists or playwrights. Yet psychosis or depression was evident in 80 percent of the poets, 80.5 percent of the novelists and 87.5 percent of playwrights. This is doubtlessly due to the fact that poets have more time on their hands: The average poem is at least 80 percent shorter than either a novel or a play, leaving the poet free to dial many emergency services in search of an audience. Novelists and playwrights, while considerably more psychotic and depressed, take it out on their characters instead, who then become models for our children when they are adapted for the screen; thus is the moral fabric of society shredded and torn.

In an unusual reversal of commonly held belief, Post found that only 31 percent of the poets were alcoholics compared to 54 percent of the playwrights. That's understandable: playwrights have more money for booze.

Half the poets, Dr. Felix found, failed to ever achieve "complete sexual union," while 42 percent of playwrights were known for their sexual promiscuity. Dr. Felix does not specify if the promiscuous playwrights achieved "complete sexual union," or whether the failing poets were promiscuous in addition to being incomplete or what happened should union occur between a poet and a playwright.

But these are small quibbles. The benefits of these findings to society are immense. Jesse Helms can now point at these figures with his cigarette and say, "See, I told you so. Cut their funds. They are nuts." Employment agencies are sure to take note. "We were thinking about hiring a poet to represent us in our negotiations with IBM, but that's out now." Next to pay attention will be landlords. "You're a playwright you say? Forty-two percent promiscuous? You'll set the dogs next door howling! Find another place!" Personally, I take Dr. Post's figures with some degree of anxiety: I write poetry and novels, and I have written plays. I must have the sorry sum of all vices and failings. Now, if only had I time enough for them!

Part Five

Amnesia of the

Body Politic

Tolerance, Intolerance,
Europe & America

There is a legend that the Pied Piper of Hamelin, who piped all the children out of Germany, piped them over the mountains to my hometown in Transylvania. It's an interesting story, I'm sure you know it. The Pied Piper of Hamelin rid the town of rats and mice by charming them away with his flute playing in the year 1284, about seven hundred years ago. When the citizens of Hamelin refused to pay him the price they agreed on, he charmed away their children in revenge.

It's an amazing story if you really think about it, which is what I do—think about stories—and I'm in good company because a lot of writers retold and thought about this story, Goethe, Browning, and the Brothers Grimm among them. What interests *me* about this story is what happened to these children after they were piped away. If indeed they were piped away to my hometown, what possibly happened to them is that they grew up into rather dour and humorless businessmen who built big walls around the city, kept very much to themselves, and traded with other people until they became rich. When they became rich, they attracted a lot of attention and were attacked by their neighbors who burned down their big houses and took their stuff. One of those who attacked was Vlad the Impaler who came to be known as Dracula, but who wasn't a vampire, only a Wallachian prince who liked to conquer places and then skewer their inhabitants on stakes. After Dracula left, the inhabitants built even bigger walls and became even more suspicious of strangers than they'd been before. They watched out for anyone who wasn't like them and either expelled them from town or killed them. In the seven hundred years that have passed since they first got to my hometown, the good citizens expelled Jews, if any of them were foolish enough to settle there, banished or tortured anyone who worshipped in a style different from their own Catholic religion, and burned witches in the town square.

In this, they were no different from the rest of their European neighbors who, in those seven hundred years, made war against each other for reasons of religion, class difference, or personal animosity. Christians made war against the Islamic Turks and against each other. Catholics made war against Protestants, one kind of Catholic made war against another kind of Catholic, one kind of Protestant made war against another kind. Anyone who challenged the official doctrines of their religious leaders was tortured and burned. The Inquisition went even further than that, and tortured and killed anyone who dared to think differently. In fact, freethinkers were viewed as more dangerous than just about anyone else, and the Inquisition made sure that ideas like "the earth revolves around the sun" were promptly squelched. Even after it became common knowledge that the earth does indeed revolve around the sun, the Church took a very long time to acknowledge that fact. Only recently did the pope say that, yes, perhaps Galileo was right and the Church wrong. But what is the value of an apology hundreds of years after the wrong? About zero, I'd say. The Church has also grudgingly acknowledged recently that Darwin may have been right, that God didn't make the earth in six days, and that, perhaps, before he made man he made something like a monkey first. Duh. Welcome to the nineteenth century, Mr. Pope! And yes, by the way, wouldn't it be nice if our own fundamentalist Christians right here in the state of Louisiana would come at least as far as the nineteenth century. Living in medieval Europe as they do is no picnic . . .

Now and then there rose among the Europeans the still-radical thought that people of different beliefs might live in peace with each other. In the mid-sixteenth century, a man named Francis David founded something called the anti-Trinitarian movement, also known as Unitarianism. Francis David wrote, "There is only one Father for whom and by whom is everything. . . . Outside of this God there is no other God, neither three nor four, neither in substance, neither in persons."

Later, Francis David taught that Jesus was a man. The son of God certainly, but not God. Normally, he would have been killed on the spot for this idea, but Transylvania, where Francis David proposed such a radical thing, was a pretty unstable place at the time. John Sigismund, the prince of the independent principality of Transylvania, ruled over a population of German Catholics and Protestants, Protestant Hungarians, Orthodox Romanians, and some Jews. The Turkish empire extracted tribute from Transylvania but it hadn't conquered it. Turkish policy did not interfere with people's religious beliefs. In that respect, Islam during the sixteenth and seventeenth centuries was much more tolerant than Christianity. Transylvania was a quintessentially multicultural region, and Prince Sigismund's rule depended on keeping this unstable religious and ethnic gumbo in a state of peaceful coexistence. Francis David's religion appealed to him. He asked the representatives of the major religions to tell him what they would do if they became the official religion of his principality. Both Catholics and Protestants answered that they would rid the country of all the others. Only Francis David said that he would let them be to worship as they pleased. And so, for a brief period of time, Transylvania became the freest, most tolerant region of Europe. When Prince Sigismund died, things reverted to their usual form. Francis David was imprisoned and tortured—and died not long after.

At just about this time, and just about when Europeans were all set on killing each other completely, the world became startlingly bigger with the discovery of America. Here, suddenly, was a place that was described by explorers as "heaven on earth," a place of bountiful riches and beauty where the Garden of Eden, inhabited by innocent and naked savages, could be found. In less than a century, Europeans populated this Garden of Eden and began killing its innocent savages, in no small part because they were "naked," which is to say, defenseless in the face of European weapons and diseases. It didn't take very long for Europeans to take their hatreds and animosities to the New World but, for reasons that I will explain later, these did not transplant as well as the bigots of the Old World might have wished.

In the nineteenth century, long after the settlement of the New World, a new religion, the most deadly yet, appeared in Europe: it was called nationalism. Different ethnic groups asserted first their independence, then their superiority over their neighbors. In the 1930s another German pied piper made his appearance and piped away a whole generation of children. This time, he wasn't satisfied to merely take them over the mountains to settle there in relative comfort. He piped them to war and by the time it was all over, in 1945, Hitler's magic flute had piped to death about one-fourth of the world's entire population. Hitler's nationalist religion was based on hatred of what he called "inferior races," particularly Jews and Slavs. Intolerance was the official state religion of Nazism, and it did not disappear with Hitler and Germany's defeat.

By the time I was born, in 1946, shortly after World War II, the adversaries had changed, but the hatreds prevailed. Instead of Catholics and Protestants and nationalists, we had communists and capitalists. The fascists had just been defeated but class struggle replaced religious intolerance. But for the quirks of Transylvanian politics I should not have been born. The Nazis certainly intended to kill my entire family because they were Jewish. But as fate would have it, they only killed half of them, the half that stayed behind in Northern Transylvania, which was occupied by pro-Nazi Hungarians. My mother, my grandmother, her sister, and her sister's husband escaped over the mountains into Romanian Transylvania on the night of the Hungarian occupation. They survived the war because the Romanians, while fascists, were not as good and as efficient at killing Jews as were the Hungarians and the Germans.

The Soviet Union liberated or occupied—depending on whom you ask—Romania in 1944. In 1947 they established a communist regime, and for the next four and a half decades, this regime did its best to eliminate anyone who questioned or disbelieved the communist ideology. My uncle Rihard, who had escaped the Nazis, ended up in a communist prison.

It became evident to us, as it had to millions of Europeans since the eighteenth century, that Europe was a nasty and unlivable place and that the ideal place to go to try to live in peace was America. We saw America as a place where one was free to believe whatever one chose. Besides, America was rich. "In America," my grandmother used to say, "dogs walk around with pretzels on their tails." Loose translation: "The sidewalks are paved with gold." But it wasn't riches that counted foremost: It was the simple and yet so complicated right to live your life without being killed for thinking or worshipping differently. This right, as we all knew, had been written into the founding of the United States of America by the constitutional Bill of Rights. Foremost among these was "the right to free speech and freedom of assembly."

This idea, originally born among the eighteenth-century revolutionaries of Europe, had taken genuine root in the New World. In 1965, following in the footsteps of millions of immigrants, my mother and I were able to obtain exit visas and head for the U.S. We arrived in New York in March 1966 and headed for Detroit, where a refugee organization sponsored us.

America was not at all like I'd imagined it. Detroit was a big, industrial city where people of different colors lived in segregated neighborhoods. The city had no cultural center where one could stroll about on foot. Everyone, it seemed, lived inside cars and drove long, exhausting miles to and from work. Some young people at that time were at war with their elders over the war in Vietnam, while the rest of young people my age were *at* war, in Vietnam. Everywhere I looked, I saw fierce and seemingly unbridgeable conflicts between people on account of their political beliefs, their race, or (surprise!) their religious beliefs. In 1967 Detroit burst into flames during a huge riot, and I saw what I had never actually seen in Romania: army tanks rumbling up the middle of the city, on Woodward Avenue, enforcing a 6 P.M. curfew with machine-gun fire. I was living in a combat zone in a neighborhood torn by strife, in a country divided by the war.

It would have been a true nightmare, if it hadn't been for something I observed right away. The *expression* of divergent points of view, no matter how different or how seemingly incompatible, was conducted publicly, without any censorship. The newspapers, the television and radio, gave every point of view a forum, and when these media became insufficient to accommodate public discourse, many people founded their own media, a so-called underground media that took public discourse to places I could barely imagine. In Romania, the press had been censored and unauthorized publishing landed one promptly in jail. And so, although I was only an immigrant, I found myself able to discuss in public matters I had only whispered about in private.

The U.S., I soon observed, was a place of tremendous diversity, as well as tension. Varying interests competed for attention with great intensity. This has been the case since the very beginning, when Alexis de Tocqueville, the Frenchman to whom we return so often when we reassess American democracy, noted, "In Europe we are wont to look upon a restless disposition, an unbounded desire for riches, and an excessive love of independence as propensities very dangerous to society. Yet these are the very elements that ensure a long and peaceful future to the republics of America."

How was it possible that unrest, civic strife, demands and counterdemands contributed not to dissolution but to greater freedoms? The sixties were an extreme time, when the contradictions that make up our society appeared in stark contrast. Life has become considerably calmer since then, but the animosities and conflicts that were revealed so dramatically back then haven't gone away.

When I first came to America, Romanian immigrants were a rarity, and immigrants, in general, were not treated with the suspicion with which they are viewed today. Differences that were acknowledged back then, though not fully tolerated, have taken on much fuller dimensions now. There is something paradoxical about this: Today, after the Cold War, the United States is the most powerful country in the world. We are enjoying a time of unprecedented prosperity. There is discussion in Congress now of huge up-coming budget surpluses, something unthinkable a few decades ago. But instead of satisfaction, American people feel anxious. Right-wing nuts blow up buildings with children in them. Religious fanatics are attempting to censor books in the library and programs on television. Racists are crawling out of the slimelight and into the limelight, blaming minorities for their own shortcomings. David Duke and Pat Buchanan want to close our borders both to immigration and to the free trade that is partly responsible for our new prosperity. The policy of human rights that was largely responsible for the collapse of the communist empire has been abandoned to the point where our president can receive a dictator like Jian Zemin of China and allow him to pronounce bold-faced lies to our Congress and press. The reason is that China wants to buy our nuclear technology and jets and, when it comes to business, human rights must take a backseat, at least to this administration. In other words, intolerance is increasing while tolerance is being paid only lip service.

On the other hand, the facts are pointing elsewhere. Immigrants are enriching this country, just as they have since they started arriving. The Chinese are reviving the economies of the inner cities, while Hispanics in California, Texas, and elsewhere are doing the jobs that Americans no longer want to perform, for wages Americans no longer accept. Business has proven now and then that flexible hours, concern for worker morale, respect for the environment, and ethical principles pay off in the long run. Tolerance for other people's religious beliefs and reasonable trust in science work to make us all better. Strong ethical stands and compassion for oppressed people still living under dictatorships gains America the gratitude of the world.

There are some who see America today breaking into myriad separate entities, into racial, sexual, generational, cultural, and linguistic ghettoes. I don't believe it. I believe that there are those who would like to see the assertion of difference as an excuse to promote their political agendas. And there are, of course, those who wish to see such breakups in order to fulfill various doomsday scenarios. And those who feel overwhelmed by the rapidity of change are using this vision as an excuse for withdrawing from public life.

Many of the arguments now used to divide us are posited in the wrong terms, the "gap" terms. Some of these gaps are real, but others are not. Take, for example, the argument between the advocates of "English only" and those promoting ethnic-language education. It shouldn't be a question of either/or. Bilingual education combined with ethnic language education makes sense. The language of the land is English—or American—so it makes sense that foreign-born residents should learn English first of all. Not to do so would condemn them to a linguistic ghetto, which would prevent them from fully joining American life. On the other hand, we should promote a partially bilingual and ethnic-language curriculum in those places where immigrants live in sizeable numbers. The fabric of America is multiracial and multicultural today. That's a fact. This is what gives this country its vitality and its substance. America is not a one-race, one-ethnicity, one-church national state of the kind that has been the cause of war in Europe for centuries. Her fabric stretches and changes. Not to admit this is a disaster. To deny education to immigrants or to promote an alienating curriculum *will* force them into linguistic ghettoes and cut off their access.

You can see the benefits not just of tolerance, but of celebrating difference, in the work of artists. The Nuyorican poets use both Spanish and English simultaneously to create rich, plastic expressions of a new kind of identity, an identity that is wholly American, not hyphenated. Their work is not the work of Puerto-Rican Americans, or Mexican-Americans, but the work of Americans, simply, the newest Americans. The same can be heard and seen in the performances of Guillermo Gomez-Pena, the work of *muralistas*, and the reflections of other émigré artists on the ambiguities of cultural translation. They all use language and other materials provocatively. The point is that we live with contradictions and absurdities in our private and political life. To look at them with candor and humor—which is to say, creatively—is to bridge them. Implicit in all viable art is the demand for everyone to be an artist. Good art makes art-communities because it speaks to the myriad gaps that are present in our lives.

Good art today is creole, mestizo, mixed, like American society. How is it still possible, after the civil-rights era, after the psychedelic age, to continue looking at things in black and white? We are no longer living in the era of the Cold War. How is it possible for some politicians to revive racism by using codes like "crime" and "IQ" to mean race? Racial purity is a myth. It is an artist's job to expose and subvert these insidious codes, as well as to thoroughly mix the palette.

The problem is not "race" or "immigration" or "free thinking" or "the media" or any of the numerous scapegoats that this country's paranoid right-wingers would like us to blame for our ills. Their solutions—censorship, repression, closing off borders, defending "patriotism" and "religion" with legislation—increase rather than diminish our difficulties. We have a reality gap in this country as big as the very real economic disparity between the poor and the rich. The discussion of social class in America has been fatally compromised of late by the ideology of capitalism-uber-alles that dominates the media and the political discourse. This obscuring has created a perfectly viable climate for hate mongers, Nazis, and other radical enemies of democracy who, in the absence of a significant discussion of class inequities, have been left in charge of the moral welfare of the dispossesed. They make up the armies of Louis Farrakhan and of the patriotic white militias.

There are those who celebrate and look for imaginative, tolerant, even loving solutions, and those who hate. The American experience shows us that we can overcome hatred, xenophobia, and fear. The European experience has shown quite the opposite. The advocates of intolerance, division, racism, and xenophobia would like us to return to the implacable hostilities of Europe. I, for one, don't believe that this is possible. The essence of America, as expressed in those sorely tested principles of the Bill of Rights, will not allow it. Unfortunately, those rights are not universally accepted even here, in the country that gave birth to them. They need to be reiterated, reaffirmed, and defended over and over. It's not a job just for the American Civil Liberties Union. It's everybody's job.

The Anxious Middle Class

ONE OF THE DEVIL'S FIELDS
OF NOUVEAU TRIUMPH

The pundits are already declaring the nineties the Age of Anxiety for the middle class. Give us a break. The middle class invented anxiety. The poor have despair and the rich have ennui. That leaves anxiety, the middling emotion. The middle class is anxious about savings, its children's future, and old age. It is this anxious middle class that Bob Dole addressed by holding before it the vision of an unanxious middle class from the fifties. Back then, the sugarplum Republican fiction goes, everybody liked Ike and women were housewives and men had lifetime jobs and big cars. That's true. Women were also on Dexedrine and Valium and highballs and got freaked out by their vacuum cleaners and frequented psychiatrists and mental hospitals. Anne Sexton, a fifties housewife, said, "Imagine it. A radio playing / and everyone here was crazy." Men were breadwinners and alcoholics and sometimes drove their big cars all the way to the edge of the continent to escape what Henry Miller called "the air-conditioned nightmare." Lest we forget, this is the generation that started the Cold War. Bob Dole's postwar middle class was wretchedly unhappy with its burden of seriousness and tedium and worry about its children, who turned into either hippies or casualties in Vietnam.

Today's middle class shouldn't be worried about its children: It should be worried about turning into the middle class of the fifties. That's a reason for anxiety! As people get older they get duller, more scared, more boring, and more frail. Despite its vaunted religiosity, American society is quite pragmatic. The past half century was ruled by four doctors: Dr. Spock, Dr. Seuss, Dr. Ruth, and now Dr. Kevorkian. The first three were Okay, but this last one makes me anxious, too. The middle-aged middle class to which I also belong fears its own evanescence: That's not anxiety, it's common sense. But there is a new ingredient to our generational anxiety that was unknown in Bob Dole's fifties: We contend with the insomniac floodlight of the news media. In the fifties the powerful made only powerful news and only the powerful made news. Now the powerful are under a microscope that reveals their every wart, which makes them just like us, which makes us anxious because we don't want them to be like us, we want them to be better. At the same time, people just like us stand mercilessly revealed on confessional television. There is nowhere to hide and this lack of privacy is anxiety-provoking indeed. You can add to that the rivers of information and the fact that the young and the hungry are better at navigating them, and we can appear quite useless to ourselves. But fear not: right below us are the poor and they are pissed. And above us are the rich and they are bored and greedy. Something's going to give.

The Angels in the Closet

I n Luis Buñuel's film *Miss Liberty,* everything we habitually share is
turned upside down. People go to the bathroom together but eat privately. Schoolboys giggle over tourist postcards as if they were pornogra-
phy. For Buñuel that was surrealism. For Americans at the end of the
twentieth century, that's just life. Everything that was in the closet is now
on TV, and everything that was publicly extolled not long ago is in the
closet.

What's a closet? Freud called it the subconscious. It was the place where
Victorians banished everything that got in the way of propriety. By the time
the Victorians got around to it, it was already crammed with everything pro-
scribed by the Church. Putting away all those matters that got in the way of
work and obedience to society had the beneficial effect of building wealth
and promoting work. By the time Freud got around to it, the closet was
bursting with our banished desires, including sex and murder. By 1914, the
closet exploded, giving birth to World War I, the Russian Revolution, the
roaring twenties, World War II, Elvis Presley, the exploding sixties, women's
liberation, and the gay movement. In between these closet-emptying events,
well-meaning men in suits tried to cram the released darkness, prurience,
lassitude, and decadent art back into the closet but that proved impossible
because the monsters grew up when they got out while the closet stayed

the same size. Or, to put it another way, the repressive apparatus of morality didn't evolve, while the hungry monsters fed and got very fat. What's kept them fat and keeps feeding them is the huge market for them. Capitalism discovered the riches within just as the markets without began shrinking.

Advertising rifles our closets for whatever might be left in them. Legitimizing our desires for the forbidden has now begun to produce a numbing effect. It is thus that the president's penis or, in Freudian terms, the father's phallus, rose into public view. There were few things that were still unthinkable. Daddy's thing was among the last. Now it's on television, and a panicked feeling grows among the marketers.

Do not fear. I am here to announce the good news. The closet is not empty. While it's true that we've taken everything formerly repressed out of it, it's been quietly filling with other furnishings, namely "the angels of our better nature," as Lincoln called them. Our desires for sublimity, excellence, genius, and moral improvement are now in the closet, furnishing the subconscious with the means to renew us.

The angels ripening in the dark will of course be very different, when they are finally released, from the virtues imagined by post-Victorians and Christian moralists. The literary canon, for instance, during its sojourn in the closet, will have no resemblance to William Bennett's canon. Nor will closet-seasoned family values resemble in the least Jerry Falwell's fondest hopes. Nor will the closet-refreshed ascetic urges have much in common with the sexual ethics promoted by various men's movements. The angels in the closet will burst upon us in the third millennium in forms unimaginable to puritans and unacceptable to zealots.

I don't know what they will look like, but I am certain that they will be paradoxical, like a young person tattooed from head to foot with the poetry of Lao Tzu or verses from the Song of Songs. The virtues of tomorrow, unlike the virtues of yore, will be inspiring shape-shifters whose purpose, in addition to saving us, will be to baffle the certainties and absolutisms of ideologues everywhere.

The reason for this optimism is that the experience of the closet will give rhetoric a rest. The public demons of today are not as mean to the closeted angels as the angels' spokespersons were to them. The prison of the subconscious is a more humane place. There is no longer such an absolute break between what's in the closet and what's on display. There is much traffic back and forth because there is now a new reality, called Virtuality, which is a bridge that unites the inside of the closet and the outside of television, our private natures and our public images. Virtuality, or VR in techno shorthand, is a purgatory, the in-between place where everything is modeled before being actualized.

Virtuality also means the the end of the respite between historical cycles of war and revolution. For the last two centuries we have had thirty to forty years of rest between explosions: Between the end of the Napoleonic wars to the revolutions of 1848, approximately thirty years; between the American Revolution and the Civil War, a hundred years divided by Indian Wars and various conflicts with Britain, Spain, and France; between the Civil War and World War I, about fifty years; between World War I and World War II about thirty years. It's been thirty years since the end of the Vietnam War. (The Korean conflict was an extension of World War II.) We seem due for another bad decade, but it won't happen. We'll have a virtual explosion, followed by the emergence from the closet of our better natures.

Of course, I may be virtually wrong.

The Devil's Most
Insidious Aspect: Amnesia

REMEMBERING ISN'T WHAT IT USED TO BE

Amnesia has settled like meteorite dust over our ever-expanding re-public. In good times, there is no need to remember. Things re-membered are usually bad, wars and traumas, public and private. Our appetite now is for distant history, dramatized hopefully in a way that makes us feel good enough to forget the more recent past. There is a scale of for-getting, from the petty to the grand, and it is all in operation now. On the petty end of the scale, take former candidate Bob Dole, for instance, who warned us, like a good Republican, against the national debt. What does he do now? Credit card commercials that urge us to increase debt. It isn't that we demand principles from politicians, it's only that we'd like them to last for at least a month after seeking public office. In the middle of the scale is Whitewater and its equivalents, dragging listlessly through the newspapers and forgotten by all but the people paid to worry them. At the grand end is the case of Secretary of State, Madeleine Albright, who claims to have only recently learned of her Jewish roots. Her parents had deliberately misled her and she cultivated amnesia.

The Hidden History of Chicago

People who like peace and quiet fare badly when the empire does well. The roar of construction machines, the resurfacing of the streets, the mushrooming of paper condos where solid brick homes once lived, the roar of blenders making "power drinks" for cell-phone holders, the grinding of espresso machines, and even the all-too-cheerful *vrroom* of the vacuum cleaner in my quaint B&B—all were loud reminders that Chicago, and America, were doing well. To the detriment of the rest of us who remember, sigh, the glories of tranquility.

My friend Anne, a young theater director, found this nice B&B for me near Halstead and Clark Streets, in a neighborhood known familiarly as "Boys Town," and soon to be named—officially—Gay Town. The name of the B& B was Villa Toscano, but far from reposing amid the peaceful hills of Tuscany, it sat between infernal roadwork machines tearing up the street.[*]

"It's the new prosperity," sighed my innkeeper. "Would you like a glass of wine? I have some excellent Merlot."

Three days before I arrived, Anne's new landlord had told her that her rent was going up $350 to "bring it in line with the market." Anne is going to move, and so are all the other artists in her building and in the neighborhood. It's an old story: Artists revive a rundown neighborhood and then develop-

---

[*]Villa Toscano, 3447 N. Halstead. Tel: 773/404-2643. Gay-friendly.

ers move in and price the artists out of their homes. Boutiques and B&Bs mushroom and the tourists pour in. It happened in New York's SoHo. It happened in New Orleans's Lower Garden District. It's happening in Chicago.

I had a plan: I wanted to avoid the obvious tourist charms of Chicago. Stay away from Michigan Avenue's Magnificent Mile. Avoid the lovely Lake Michigan beaches. Set foot in none of the grand museums. No ethnic festivals, those orgies of faux-peasant cuteness that abound in the Midwest. No cultural events "under the Picasso," which are city-sponsored affairs to promote optimism. Eat in none of the nouveau eateries. Touch no arugula.

Around the world, Chicago is known for three things other than those listed above: Al Capone's mob, Chicago blues, and the Labor Struggle. I wasn't up for the Capone tour because I'd sort of lost interest when Geraldo Rivera opened the gangster's vault and found nothing inside. As for the blues, we have them at home in New Orleans, and I hear them all the time.

What I hoped to see were the sites commemorating Chicago's long and distinguished history of labor struggle. How did this "broad-shouldered city," "hog-butcher to the world," as Carl Sandburg called it, remember its past? How did it commemorate the Haymarket Riot? The Pullman Strike? The Steel Massacre of 1937? The Chicago Democratic Convention of 1968? Chicago had been a vast laboratory for progressive ideas. It had shaped America. I wanted to see the places where this history had taken place, and I was curious to see if there was still a radical Chicago where these ideas continued to be debated. Ideas, unlike buildings, are never finished.

Danny Postel was just the man for the job. The young editor of the journal *Lip*, was an enthusiast.* The latest *Lip* featured such articles as, "What, Me, Racist?," an interview with antiracist activist Tim Wise, "America's Indonesian Killers," and "My Day as a Dominatrix." That seemed radical enough for me, and my guide made sure that I was not disappointed. He picked me up at the Villa Toscano, and for the next two days we covered what felt like one thousand miles, visiting radical Chicago history past and present.

"The South Side," Danny declared grandly, "is the cradle of Chicago civilization. Totally below the radar. No mention by the tourist bureau." In fact, so little mention was made of it that one Rand McNally map of Chicago,

---

Lip, edited by Brian Basel and Danny Postel and distributed by Left Bank Distribution, 1404 18th Ave., Seattle, WA 98122.

the "Easy Finder," did not even have the South Side on it. The El train, which used to service the South Side, had been removed. An iffy bus system took its place.

Our first destination on the South Side was a factory building in Hyde Park. Here, Danny told me, some of Chicago's most serious radicals labored on a number of projects. The building was near the steam plant of the University of Chicago, but finding the entrance was not so easy. After circling the massive brick structure several times, we entered through an open door into a crowded wood shop. A carpenter in there turned off his saw and explained that the shop was one of many community-based projects in the factory. All the wood was scavenged from demolitions and the loose boards were turned into furniture. He guided us through piles of boards and unfinished bookcases to a bicycle shop. Hundreds of cannibalized bicycles shared space here with chairs made out of tire tubes and wheel frames. I sat in one and it was very comfortable. This business was run by poor neighborhood children who came here to work on bicycles for themeselves and for resale. Like the woodshop, it was part of something called the Resource Center, an organization dedicated to recycling and community activism.* On the other side of the bike shop, we met three Danish young men who asked us if we wanted to see the Superflex. I didn't see why not.

The Superflex, which they had brought with them from Denmark, was a plastic ball that sat in the middle of an empty loft with pipes coming out of it.** Inside the ball, a combination of organic materials, such as dung and agricultural waste, produced "biogas," a cheap form of energy capable of heating and lighting a house. The Danes were on a world tour to promote biogas. Some of their Superflex balls were already operating in subequatorial Africa, lighting up hundreds of homes.

"Biogas plants are built by dreamers for poor people," Bjorg explained simply.

We invited them to tour radical Chicago with us.

We climbed a perilous staircase and arrived in an office filled to the rafters with books and manuscripts. This had been our destination all along.

---

*Blackstone Ave. Bicycle Works, 6100 S. Blackstone Ave., Chicago, IL 60637. Tel. 773/241-5458.
**For more information on the Superflex, find them online at *www.superflex.dk* or e-mail them *superflex@superflex.dk.*

Here was the editorial office of *The Baffler*.* Tom Frank, one of the editors, was a distinguished historian and writer who, like Danny, consented to be a guide. The latest issue of *The Baffler* was itself a radical site. The theme was "The Folklore of Capitalism." There was an article on Sinclair Lewis and eternal Babbitry, an exposé of Amway, and an analysis of working-class amnesia that proved, beyond a shadow of doubt and with charts, that today's workers remember nothing of the past of the labor movement.

Tom was a maelstrom of activity with round professorial glasses. Before we could start our tour, he insisted on watering his garden plot behind the building. He was growing cabbages, brussels sprouts, lettuce, and tomatoes. The plot was one of several in a large community garden tended by poor folk from the South Side who often had barbecues and get-togethers here. While Tom watered he explained that the South Side was still safe from the frenzy of urban renewal that had seized other parts of Chicago.

"Too many poor people," he laughed.

We commandeered the van of the Danes and headed for the East Side, toward some of the mightiest steel mills of America. They were mostly silent now, victims of the seventies depression in the steel industry. Their looming hulks were surrounded by high fences. We passed the huge abandoned high-rises of the Robert Taylor Homes, the largest housing project outside the former USSR. They were in the process of being demolished.

"Where are the people going to live?" asked Bjorg.

Danny and Tom both shrugged. Danny said, "Nobody cares about that." Tom added, "The rich are taking back their city."

Tom pointed out the vacant lot and park where the famous World's Fair of 1893 had taken place. A forlorn gold statue of a woman without any identification rose stiffly from an intersection.

"All that's left," said Tom, "She's supposed to represent Progress or something."

We passed through neighborhoods named Hegewisch and Pilsen, once German, Czech, and Polish enclaves, now mostly Mexican. The idle steel mills framed the houses like dead volcanoes. Police cars went by, sirens blaring. An immense car graveyard flashed by. Finding Republic Steel, where the Massacre of 1937, had taken place was not easy. We drove around and

---

The Baffler, edited by Thomas Frank and Greg Lane, P.O. Box 378293, Chicago, IL 60637.

around, until Tom, who had visited and written about the place, spotted Avenue O. There, at the intersection of Avenue O and 115th Street, was the driveway for Republic Steel.[*]

A grassy area with listing benches surrounded a curious steel sculpture shaped like a lopped-off pyramid with some strands of stiff metal spaghetti rising out of it.

"This is it," Tom said.

There was no "it," since there was nothing written on the object to indicate what it was for. But at this very spot, in 1937, the company's security had opened fire at a picnic by striking workers and killed ten of them as they attempted to flee. The massacre caused outrage around the world and led to changes in the industry.

Site One on the Tour of Uncommemorated History.

We drove over the Calumet River, past more hulking reminders of an industrial past that was irretrievably gone. A few barges rusted in an industrial canal. White gypsum piles rose on the banks. A sign painted on an overpass said TRAINING THE COMMUNITY ON TOURISM. Right.

We reached Pullman, a company town that had been wholly owned by George Pullman, the maker of luxury railroad cars.[**] In Pullman's paternalistic town, workers were lodged and fed, with rents and food deducted from their paychecks. The town was segregated by class: the foremen lived in the bigger houses on the outer edge of the town. There was a grocery store, a bank, a general store, a post office. Things were going well until the depression of 1893, when Pullman began laying off workers and cutting wages. The Railroad Workers Union entered the scene under the leadership of Eugene V. Debs, a young labor leader who went on to become one of the founders of the Socialist Party. The resulting strike and the sympathy strikes that followed came the closest to a general strike ever in the United States. When Pullman's appeals to the Illinois National Guard to crush the strike failed, President Cleveland authorized the use of federal troops. It was the first federal intervention in a labor dispute. The Pullman Strike, known also

---

[*]Republic Steel and Uncommemorated Site of the Steel Massacre of 1937, Ave. O and 115th St.

[**]Pullman Historic District, northeast corner of 112th Street and Cottage Grove Avenue. Hotel Florence Restaurant & Museum claims to be open Monday through Sunday for lunch, but it wasn't when we visited.

as the Debs Revolt led to Debs's jailing and his defense by the young Clarence Darrow, who later became famous for his defense of evolution teaching in the Scopes Trial. Debs ran for the presidency from jail and got one million votes.

So much history! The Pullman Historic District, a quaintly renovated area with a small hotel and a friendly park, gave no hint of any of it. The Florence Restaurant and Hotel was closed. There were four holes in a gray slab of stone where a plaque had been removed. There was a social-realist mural of some happy workers, but otherwise there were no other markers or monuments of any kind. A few brochures lying about in dusty boxes outside the hotel made short shrift of the Pullman Strike, choosing to emphasize instead the quaintness of the surroundings. Tom was distressed. He had visited Pullman two years before and, at that time, the hotel had been open. It looked as if even the nonthreatening history was in danger of disappearing.

"It says that we are in Pullman but we are not," Tom said pensively. The remark could have stood for all of the Chicago history we were trying to visit. We were in Chicago but we were not.

An old man walking his dog stopped and looked at our bewildered little group. "Anything you want to know?"

I asked him if anyone remembered the Pullman Strike, maybe from his father's or grandfather's stories.

"I'm 83 years old. I know about it. But the young'uns seventy or so, they just watch the TV." His name was Mr. Ed Berger, and that's all he'd say.

The Danes were pretty amazed. "In Denmark we have plaques and statues for everything," said Bjorg, who seemed to be the spokesman for the group. The other Danes were taciturn but they nodded in agreement nonetheless.

The next stop was the site of the Haymarket Riot of 1886.* On the third of May of that year, an unknown person threw a bomb just as policemen were trying to break up a mass meeting where anarchists were speaking. In the ensuing riot, both demonstrators and policemen were killed. Eight anarchists were arrested and condemned for the bombing on very little evidence. Four of them were hanged in 1887. The execution aroused the anger

---

*Randolph and Desplaines Streets.

of revolutionaries around the world. May Day, the International Workers' Day, began as a commemoration of Haymarket. It is now celebrated everywhere in the world except in the United States, where Labor Day is not in May. In 1889 the city of Chicago commemorated the event with a statue in honor of the policemen killed, depicting a helmeted officer with his hand raised over the inscription, "In the name of the people of Illinois, I command peace." One year after the Chicago riots at the Democratic Convention in 1968, an underground radical group, the Weathermen, blew up the statue. It was restored and returned to its pedestal, only to be blown up exactly one year later on the same anniversary. Only the pedestal remained, but in 1996, Mayor Richard Daley, Jr., the son of the elder Daley who battled the demonstrators in 1968, had this last reminder of Haymarket removed so as not to mar the view to the new convention center.

We stood around the rippled slab of stone where all this history had taken place, looking at one another.

"This was the place?" Bjorn asked rhetorically.

Below us, a busy freeway rushed its commuters into the suburbs, none of them any wiser that just over their heads a small group of unconventional tourists was trying to figure out just what it was about its own history that still gave Chicago nightmares.

The Haymarket Riot was not entirely uncommemorated: a few blocks away, by an empty parking lot, a square bronze plaque about the size of a pizza carton was embedded in the sidewalk. Inscribed on it was a confusing story that would have seriously baffled anyone not already fully cognizant of the events.

We loitered around Unremarked Site Number Three for a while, not quite sure what to do. "I'm baffled," I said.

"So are we all," said Tom. "That's why we call our magazine *The Baffler*."

There was only one person in Chicago with the power to unbaffle us. This was a man who was a historical monument himself, the writer Studs Terkel. Born in 1912, Studs Terkel had interviewed thousands of ordinary folk and spokesmen for ordinary folk, and had warmly defended the waning light of American progressive thought for over half a century. His books include the celebrated *Hard Times: An Oral History of the Great Depression*, and *Working: People Talk About What They Do All Day And How They Feel About It*.

Studs's office was in the building of the Chicago Historical Society, where he holds the title of senior researcher. We found the building but it turned out that Studs's office, like all the other hidden history of Chicago, wasn't so easy to find. We wandered around for a time with a baffled security guard, before we found the door. On the other side of it, an intelligent man with a wild shock of white hair and sparkling eyes full of wit bade us welcome.

The writer divined what I had come to ask him before I even opened my mouth. "You want to know about forgetting," he said. "The children and grandchildren of the men and women who were saved by the New Deal are now voting to cut funding to schools and aid for the poor. How could they have forgotten? I'll tell you. They forgot because it is America's business to make them forget. The Cold War changed everything. The language changed. We are suffering from national Alzheimer's disease. Trivia is news now. Everything's been trivialized. Once upon a time Hannah Arendt said that the Nazis proved 'the banality of evil.' We are now living through the evil of banality."

The old master of the word smiled ruefully as he reminisced about his friend Nelson Algren, about intellectual publications like *The Anvil* and *The Spectator,* and about tumultuous and challenging times when ideas were alive. He raged against corporate downsizing and the so-called prosperity.

Several times I tried to say something and Studs kindly put in his hearing aid to listen. But when it became obvious that all I wanted was to urge him to keep talking, he took it out and did just that, like a luminous fountain, still full of passion and guts. Ah, history! Here at last was a living monument of everything prosperous Chicago tried hard to forget. Studs Terkel knew about that, too.

"It's funny. They used to blacklist me. Now I'm an icon. Live long enough and everything happens!"

I hope so. Chicago has done a pretty good job of forgetting, but then here is Studs Terkel. And Danny Postel of *Lip.* And Tom Frank of *The Baffler.* And four Danes. And, doubtlessly, many others, even as they keep migrating from their condo-fied apartments into cheaper places that aren't even on the map.

Our last visit was to an artist named Marcos Raya, a muralist who lives in the Chicano barrio. His murals, depicting revolutionary scenes of Chicano life, adorn several walls. In his studio, there is the intense activity of a man always working. But his greatest pleasure, he said, "was to live among my people here in the barrio. I don't want to be in a condo or loft in a hip part of town. All my life I lived and painted here with working people. This is a neighborhood."

Marcos's apartment and his murals are live monuments.* Chicago may not note and mark its radical past, but it should pay close attention to the present.

---

*You can see some of Marcos Raya's murals in the vicinity of West 19th Street.

Shell Games

I squeezed in next to a corporate fixer on a flight back to New Orleans. I tried to prop up my laptop on the food tray but the seat in front of me reclined and I was nearly killed by my laptop. The fixer said, "You need to get a smaller laptop," and I said, "We need to have better airlines!" and therein lay a vast philosophical difference between us. There are those who'd defend corporations to the death, right down to their right to make dogfood out of us, and those, like myself, who think human beings come first, and corporations second. The fixer's job was, as he put it, "information architecture," which is to say, redesigning corporate structure to minimize inefficiency, maximize productivity, and squeeze out dead time. Worthy goals, so I asked him if our current prosperity was fueled by the efficiency of the new information technologies. Not at all, he said. Our current prosperity is due to speculation, inflated estimates, rosy forecasts, and manipulation of the financial markets. There isn't a blessed thing being created, it's all paper profits. Everyone is in debt, and the gap between rich and poor is growing. Well, those were my sentiments exactly, but it was strange to hear them come from the lips of a corporate savior. How is the illusion maintained? I wanted to know. Shell games, he said. Everybody is busy getting frequent flier miles, playing with credit cards, filling out coupons, hoping to be the first to reach Gold status in something or other. It's one huge game of trying to find the pea under the walnut shell. Meanwhile, the big boys go on extorting time. For every corporate minute gained, there are a thousand human minutes lost. Do you think anyone works eight hours a day anymore? he asked. Not a chance. Everyone works from sunrise till well past midnight, if you count all the time spent on the computer or watching television, which is all work. Television isn't entertainment, it's advertising setting you up for the weekend shopping spree. So, I said, I'm right we need better airlines, not smaller computers and tinier bodies? Yeah, you're right, he said, but so what? The airline's come up with a new gambling gimmick—the whole country's gambling-crazy—and you'll never notice yourself shrinking. You'll never even think of complaining. You might be losing frequent flier miles.

Prosperity and the Devil

I am writing this on October 16, 1998, and I cannot hear myself think. There are cranes, bulldozers, and maniacal contractors swarming all over America, making infernal noises. I haven't had a quiet moment since the demon Prosperity landed in the USA. Even in New Orleans, the last place on earth you might think such a demon would inhabit! Of course, it being New Orleans, Prosperity takes on peculiar forms.

The maniac next door has been banging on my wall for six months now. He's rebuilding a nineteenth-century house the nineteenth-century way, which is to say with little iron scrapers and chisels. If guys like this had their way, we'd do everything like we did in the nineteenth century. Wars with trenches and bayonets. Boiling laundry on the woodstove. Nice epidemics. Incurable TB. Nostalgia is masochism and masochism is something masochists love to share. It would be okay if all these lovers of the past kept their suffering to themselves. But their self-righteous banging makes the rest of us suffer. And that's when we turn sadistic. The thing is, all the scraping and spooning of precious old dirt has been sending the French Quarter rats in search of quieter abodes. So they're moving next door. That's right. Into my house. Well, the plan is this: I have a powder that drives rats crazy: It makes them nostalgic for their home and they grow enraged at those who disturbed them. So they go back and eat the nostalgia guy down to his littlest bones. Ah!

192

But like I said, things could be worse. Chased out of my lair by the lovers of the past, I am penning these poison-pen tropes at the open window of Café Kaldi on a splendid blue day. The sounds of the swing band across the street at the French Market Café drift in. Three living tableaux, tattooed with the psychedelic minutiae of a strife-free world, just ambled by and dissolved in brightness. A skinny fellow with a small red Mohawk and Elton John sunglasses is pulling a stubborn bulldog puppy by a sequin-studded leash. A delivery man is pulling a handcart full of Turbodog beer into the delivery door of a restaurant on Calle San Felipe, as the elaborate faience plaque on the wall identifies St. Philip Street. There are no big trucks, because they aren't allowed here. A mule-drawn carriage just went by slowly, the lone muleteer nearly asleep under his straw hat. The air is redolent of shrimp and sweet olive.

The thing is, I like the nineteenth century, and parts of the eighteenth. I'm even fond of small portions of the seventeenth. That's why I live in New Orleans, in the French Quarter. It's the only place in America I know of where you don't need a car, where you can walk out any hour of the night and find natives at work in the ditches of bohemia. But the thing is, it's easier to maintain the nineteenth century with twentieth-century tools. Easier and faster. You can have the pleasures of the past without vermin, scurvy, and rusted wall scrapers. Please say it's so, and I'll call back the rats.

Please give me back the peace and quiet of a mild recession. I want to hear things rust! Demons do not hatch in silence. They hatch in the optimistic din of well-being.

Houses and Shops

The French Quarter of New Orleans is the most mysterious neighborhood in America. The seveteenth- and eighteenth-century Spanish houses hide behind their high walls, impenetrable to the casual onlooker. A rich and secret life takes place behind them, in patio gardens, along second- and third-story galleries, and in tall, fan-cooled rooms. Slavery, murder, abjection, romance, and the discussion of the opera is what used to take place. Nowadays, those horrors have transmuted into other, less spectacular activities, such as lawyer orgies. Many is an attorney who sheds his and her strict redingote for the orchid silk of the afterhour bathrobe in the Vieux Carré. Real estate is so pricey in this unique corner of America that lawyers are being followed by Hollywood moneybags in search of fantasy and escape. For the newcomers, the Quarter must adhere strictly to the Church of Restoration, which is the new high religion of the South, from Savannah to New Orleans. Alas, many of the local Realtors, out for a buck, are turning the insides of historic buildings into Highway 66 motel rooms, complete with shag, Formica, and bathrooms from Home Depot. The reason for this evil work is that apartments thus appointed rent for considerable prices to yet another class of newcomers, the suburban escapees. These creatures like their façades historic but their insides square.

It's so hot these days, the sweat runs down the windows of antique shops and down the backs and fronts of New Orleanians, some of whom are secretly happy because, eyes half-closed, they are guiding the path of a sweat drop to rich and giddy places. It's all in the management of sweat, trust me. At any given time, a drop is heading somewhere. Which explains the utter lack of thought as I stroll through the French Quarter noting that houses are old shops and shops are new houses. This is a universal rule: Everything that used to be in shops is now inside people's houses. You can find all the old shops in people's houses here. But in most of America, the river of household items has been swelling decade after decade through mass-production, and it's only obsolescence that keeps it moving. The old shops are still intact in the old Quarter houses, many of which have been antique shops several times already. The point of this is that everyone lives in a shop. In the old days people lived in small shops and there were fewer of them. The new people live at Wal-Mart and there are millions of them. Houses used to turn into shops but no longer: now houses just fall apart and the shops are all new. Only shops turn into houses now, a one-way flow with no end in sight. Except in the Vieux Carré, where the nude lawyers roam, and Realtors smoke cigars.

From American Life

Two new establishments have opened in the neighborhood, both of them emblematic of a new status quo in America. The first is a cigar café, with a few tables and a number of humidors where for a few hundred dollars a year you can keep your cigars moist. The humidors are like safety-deposit boxes, with your name on them. Whenever you're ready to entertain, you bring your client or your pal here, pull out your smokes and puff away. The other day, two young urban types of the late nineties, wearing East Coast collegiate garb ca. 1956, were obscuring each other with smokescreen while a black jazz trio was entertaining them at a discreet distance, which in New Orleans is about twenty inches. The doors of the cigar café were open, letting in the ninety-five-degree heat and hair-curling humidity, but the cool inherent in the whole mode was such that the smokers remained glacial while the performers sweated rivers in strict compliance with cliché. Cigars have been around for a while, representing the new Republican ethos, which is to say a nostalgia for a time of no taxes, no labor unions, silk-lined overcoats, top hats, and the pursuit of actresses. In New Orleans, one sees the longest cigars protruding out of the well-rounded lips of short, fat guys accompanied by tall leggy girls whose profession was once described as "out-of-work actress."

The other establishment, which is no less pertinent, is a dog bakery situated in splendidly lit rooms filled with barrels of dog treats, spotless vitrines full of dog pastries, and displays of pies and cakes for special doggy anniversaries. The counter sports a few stools to one side where the dog owners, who come in ultrachic fashions, can sip a glass of Merlot while choosing among the pricey treats. Dog pastries are not cheap, mind you. They cost about the same as human pastries, but they are made without the salt and sugars that, the sales girl explained, are detrimental to canine health. The clientele at the dog bakery—and the place is mobbed!—consists of young and not-so-young women who squire a bewildering variety of pooches to the joint. The other day, a near-riot occurred when a dogcatcher van stopped and scooped up a pricey barkum from the rich crop in front of the store. Incensed owners poured out from inside, surrounded the van, and threatened to overturn it and to set the dogcatcher on fire. Sensibly, the man surrendered the coiffed lifeform and was able to drive away.

The dog-ladies are, it seems to me, the natural mates of the cigar-chompers across the street. Their belief is that their dogs defend them from crime, but stylishly, because the dogs, in addition to eating pastries, are pedigreed and come, formally, in every shape from accordion pleats to taut mauves. The cigar smokers dream of an economy where such luxuries are affordable, and safety does indeed come in many shapes. Meanwhile, the band plays on, the dogcatcher is on the run, the market is on the rise, and the heat means nada to the cool.

Fried Rice

New Orleans is an operetta-type town, and we've had one of the best lately. Anne Rice, the vampire queen, publicly attacked Al Copeland, the fried chicken king, over a matter of taste. Ms. Rice took out a full-page ad in the *New Orleans Times-Picayune* complaining about the garish architecture of Copeland's new Streja restaurant on St. Charles Avenue. Copeland, the creator of the Popeye Chicken franchise, has transformed a used-car dealership into a pastel pastry that sits smack in the middle of a nearly abandoned section of the famous Avenue. Ms. Rice, who owns several houses around a much ritzier section of the Avenue, felt the calling of something civic and something aesthetic in her blood. She has expressed herself in paid ads before, most recently in order to tell us who to vote for in the presidential election, but this time she hit hot grease. Al Copeland slammed right back with a paid ad in which he extolled the architectural virtues of his "California-Creole" restaurant and threatened to sue the irate inkster. The newspaper first headlined the fight COPELAND FRIES RICE, then conducted a public survey whereby three thousand New Orleanians faxed, e-mailed, and wrote in their opinions; 75 percent of them favored Al Copeland for bringing economic improvment to the area, while a considerably more subdued 25 percent defended Ms. Rice's cri de sang. At Mardi Gras, a whole brigade of revelers appeared wearing plates of rice and beans around their waists, promoting a dish they called Red Beans Anne Rice, though it was somewhat unclear whose side they were on. The people of New Orleans take both fried food and gothic writing seriously, but this time architecture was involved and the feeling was almost French. The fight between the Queen of Vampires and the King of Kitsch is already drawing promoters and bookies, and there is speculation that the citizens intend to see this resolved in the traditional Creole manner, mano a mano in a mud-wrestling pit. The New Orleans courts, while often resembling mud-fighting pits, are too dry a venue for the roused appetites of this city. The rumor mill claims that Anne Rice is on the verge of opening a vampire restaurant called Café Lestat right in the neighborhood of Streja, in which case there will be street battles between fanged fanciers of blood puddings and Shirley Temples and Americans going for chicken and Cokes. If any blood is spilled there will be no shortage of vampires to lap it up. Culture moves forward, and the cause of silliness is greatly advanced.

Marcel Duchamp Would've
Loved Wal-Mart

M arcel Duchamp, who turned a toilet bowl and the art world upside down, would have loved Wal-Mart. What this French artist,
who saw deeper and more ironically than a thousand art critics
with pigeons on their shoulders, called "ready-mades" in 1913 is off the
charts aesthetics-wise in 1999. The toilet bowl is a mud hut compared to
the skyscraping barbecue moon-units on sale now. The lines, the curves, the
gleam, the aerodynamics, the embarrassment of rich formal play—who designs these things anyway? Duchamp would've taken a huge nap in this suburban cathedral: Art has become both automatic and inevitable. Turn up
the gleaming fan, draw the miniblinds!

Obviously, humans don't design these things any longer: machines design
themselves. Humans used to be tool-users, but now tools are human-users.
Life used to adapt to the natural environment, but now the technological
environment adapts humans to its own purposes. The price for becoming
functioning adaptations of a virtual environment is our humanity. Is that a
big deal? Most of us have grown gradually used to being appendages of machines, so we barely notice it any more. But take these villagers in Alaska:

An AP dispatch from Arctic Village, Alaska, details the disappearance of
a whole way of caribou-hunting life beginning in January, 1980, the day a
TV set landed in this village. From that day on, the Eskimos never stopped

watching television, "learning what has been missing from their lives: Denim wear. Farberware. Tupperware. Four-wheelers. Touch-tone phones. Can openers. Canned peaches. Cabinets (for all the cans)." Outside, the snow is littered as far as you can see with "empty Chef Boyardee tins, bales of fiberglass insulation, Hills Bros. coffee cans, shotgun casings, plastic Pepsi bottles . . ." Gone are all the things Wal-Mart never carried, such as the local Eskimo language, beaded moccasins, caribou jerky, caribou-skin kayaks, caribou songs, and caribou dances.

It took TV just a few years to move people out of the Arctic to the inside of Wal-Mart. The Arctic used to be spare, all classical lines, nothing wasted, the people arrow-sharp, adapted like whalebone harpoons to the elements. They were sharp and proud and now they are soft and captive and kitsched to the max.

Now and then a crank tries to escape, like Sigurdur Hjartarson from Reykjavik, the founder of the Phallological Museum where he is going to exhibit at least one specimen of the penis of every mammal native to Iceland or its waters. Right now he's got eighty-two of them, either dried on wall mounts or pickled in preserving jars, including those of fifteen whales. Hjartarson opened his museum in 1977, three years before the Eskimos in Arctic Village got their first TV. Some three thousand visitors have come so far, to see how nature used to design things. Marcel Duchamp might have gotten up from his nap to visit the Phallological Museum, but then he would have gone right back to sleeping at Wal-Mart. Objects reproduce more aesthetically.

Mystery of the Market

For many years now, I have kept a list of what I call Insoluble Mysteries. These are things I will never understand no matter how hard I exercise my limited abilities. On this list there are Grand Insoluble Mysteries, Middling Insolubles, and Petit Insolubles. God, for instance, is at the top of the Grand Insolubles. When I address the Divinity, I call it Your Mysteriousness, but mostly I don't because such perfect obscurity renders me both humble and speechless. This is the proper stance before a Grand Insoluble, though people, being people, will talk anything to death, even God. There aren't many Insolubles on this scale, but in the middling and petit categories there are hundreds: trigonometry, the world's fascination with Elvis, the stock market, the stupidity of television, tourism, politicians, fried cheese, Muzak, North Korea. These little mysteries grow and shrink over time. One mystery lately growing in insolubility is the stock market. While I don't think that it will ever reach the status of a Grand Insoluble, the market is nonetheless cause for major wonder. Why in the world does it fall every time there is good news? Aren't stock marketeers Americans like the rest of us? Shouldn't they be happy that unemployment is down, that people are working, making a living, maybe even getting a little extra to invest in the stock market? I can see why the North Koreans might be happy if we had unemployment and starvation over here, because then they could tell their people that capitalism is inhuman. Is the stock market North Korean? I've heard it said that what makes the market so anti-American is fear of inflation, because if people have more money they'll spend it on the very products the market bets on and that will make the products more expensive and the money less valuable. But if nobody buys the products, where is the profit? I just don't get it. The market will never be a Grand Insoluble because its weirdness has no grandeur. Most Middling and Petit Insolubles have this in common: Their mysteriousness is nauseating, not awesome.

From Subversion to Whimsy

The whole of the US of A is feeling so damn good these days you wonder where all the sick, poor, and malcontent are hiding. There is no unemployment, Wall Streeters' pockets are bulging with dollars, Beverly Hillers are throwing hundred-thousand-dollar bar mitzvahs for their thirteen-year-olds, and first-class seats on airplanes are harder to find than Cuban cigars. In this forest of well-being and flushed cheeks, only the merest little whispers of dissent break the happy news. I would like to draw your attention to two of these, because of their good-natured character and non-threatening nature.

An outfit in Belgium launched a pie attack on Bill Gates as part of what they call "a pie war on all the unpleasant celebrities in every domain." They have pied, among others, the French writer Marguerite Duras who, they say, "represents the empty novel." They have a long list of these "empty" figures, but they admit that there are so many of them "there are not enough pies in all of Belgium" for all of them. While one cannot deny the satisfaction of seeing Bill Gates's bland-boy mug with Belgian cream all over it, the pie-ing itself is such a benign Groucho-Marxist-anarchist activity that I, for one, don't know whether to laugh or cry. The world has gone as flat as a pie on a television screen. Everything proceeds from the media, toward the media, and out of the media. If any critique of our way of happiness exists outside the media, you can be sure that we'll never hear about it. "Imagine," said Larry King, "You're the pope, you're Castro, and one day there is nobody there, they've all gone to see Monica Lewinsky. You get a phone call from God and one from Monica's lawyer. Who would you choose? Monica, Monica." And that's the way it is. Not enough pies in Belgium.

Another subversive outfit going by the name RTmark™ has declared April 6 World Phone-In-Sick Day. On that day, you're supposed to call in sick in order to "encourage resistance." I'm all for it. I hope I feel well on April 6 because I always call in sick when I feel good. What's the point in going to work if you're feeling well? And if everybody in the world feels well, according to the statistics, what's the point of going to work? I suspect, however, that the opposite is true: Everybody in the world feels sick and it's only Prozac, work, Bill Gates, and the media that keep us from realizing it. What is one to do with the recent report from Second Harvest that one in every ten Americans is going to seek help from a food bank this year? Where are all these starving people coming from? Eastern Europe? RTmark bills itself as a "sponsor of intelligent sabotage and subversion," but those are big words in these days of capitalism-uber-alles. Sabotage is lemon meringue and subversion just a form of whimsy. Let's face it. We live inside a programmed dream only God can wake us up from. But Monica's lawyer is on the phone. Not enough pies in Belgium.

Heat and the
School for Crawling

I t's summer in New Orleans, the season of heat and wetness that no civilian can imagine. But to us, veterans, it is the season of alligator-deep dreams, the hour of archetypal mud-shapes that crouch at the bottom of our groggy souls. To walk through this wet shimmer takes both grace and grimness. True natives, a lovely native told me, do not sweat, they glisten. We are going to open a school to teach the management of sweat: There will be classes in Glistening, in Single Sweat-Drop Control, in Walking for Ecstasy. Yes, you can walk for ecstasy if you know just how and where to direct those salty beads wrenched from your body by the heat.

There is madness in heat, as the Indian subcontinent's nuclear tests prove. It's hot in India, as hot as it is in New Orleans, and when heat-madness strikes, the tendency is to create more heat, annihilating heat. The Indian and Pakistani atom bombs are the insane thoughts of the heat-driven. People in the tropics have quick tempers. The sun is an unending test site of nuclear explosions. There is an urgent need in such regions to constantly assert the self, which is constantly dwarfed by the sun and liquefied by the heat. Nationalism is a heat disease, one of many, as humanity's long, hot summers, and bright, short explosions strive to illustrate over and over.

Our School for Sweat Management will teach more than the aesthetics of living covered in hot dew drops. We will have such classes as Tropical

Temper Management, How to Deal with Heat under the Collar, What To Do Instead of Blowing Something up When You Feel That Only Blowing Something up Will Do. We will teach Coolness, Even Temper, the Practical Uses of a Refrigerated Cucumber, the Poetry of Arbian, the snow poet. You will graduate from this school with a degree in Pleasure & Diplomacy and will qualify for summer vacations in New Orleans.

Did I forget anything? Yeah, my deodorant.

Ice

I saw an ice-covered pond in Ypsilanti, Michigan. It was awesome. I'd forgotten about ice. It's this transparent, blue-gray surface with a network of intricate rippled cracks. I felt immensely nostalgic as a whole past life spent in wintery regions came back to me. I grew up in the mountains of Transylvania, where mothers still pull their children and their groceries in sleds on iced-over streets. I remembered walking across rivers that were deep and agitated in the summer but were perfectly still and confined for the winter months. I remembered skating and skidding across polished puddles on my way to school. I recalled the slight twinge of anxiety when, as a child, I walked past dagger-sharp ten-foot icicles hanging from the eaves of buildings, ready to plunge down and impale me. Only a few years ago, in Chicago, two men were pierced through the heart by ice daggers falling simultaneously from high-rises. It happens several times every winter in every northern city, but mostly in Chicago where the fancy architecture promotes and shelters the deadliest shivs. I lived for a time in Detroit, where the front door of your building freezes like a metal pond, and the only antidotes are sleeping for three months with a saucy mate and a large cat, a spigot of hot chocolate, and the early poetry of Leopold Senghor. I also lived in New York, where huge drifts of snow rendered the city as still as a mountain village and as dreamy as a pillow. In Bucharest in 1990, a few days after the revolution that toppled the communist regime, the streets turned to ice, and the terrorists still fighting for the old order froze in their underground tunnels and turned into statues. The people broke them up with hammers and slid home clutching a frozen chunk of terrorist to turn into mantelpiece art. Today, every household in Bucharest sports an ice-covered fragment of secret policeman in the living room and there is a general belief that the old order could be restored any coming winter if enough people put their chunks together. It's a jigsaw puzzle no one wants to see executed.

Here in the subtropics we use ice for entertainment. Blocks of ice covered in straw were delivered to homes in New Orleans until early in this century, while young damsels clad in ice-cream shifts chewed flirtatiously on slivers of ice in coffeehouses decorated with frescoes of Russian ice palaces. Ice was the acme of chic. One of the most famous passages in a novel is the opening of Gabriel García Márquez's tropical saga, *One Hundred Years of Solitude,* where Colonel Buendia, about to be executed by a firing squad, remembers the day he discovered ice. Here, we cram our drinks with ice cubes, a habit that so horrifies Parisian waiters they refuse requests from Americans for "more ice," because they believe, as do most winter people, that too many ice cubes in your drink cause pneumonia. It was an outlaw New Orleanian, Pierre Moudrais, who started calling diamonds "ice," and it was another New Orleanian, Governor Claiborne, who first quipped about being "iced" in lieu of "buying the farm." The Florida poet Alcee Perrot wrote, "Ice is hard and cold and hell's horror / this is why it is our mirror." Ms. Alcee Perrot had been born in Canada, where she had been made to dig holes in an icy lake by her father, a trapper and fisherman. After running away from home with a bohemian strongman for a small circus and settling in Tallahassee, she wrote home: "I'm not longing for darkness, thick fur, and windwept snow over frozen lakes, and I'm never coming home, Papa." She became, as she put it in another of her mediocre sonnets, "a fleur of moisture and heat / an orchid perhaps or a squid." She never wrote a Dostoyevskian novel, but then she lived a long life and helped end this column with a poetic snowflake.

Hint of Fall

Most of you, used to big fat red and yellow leaves and brisk winds smelling of apples, wouldn't recognize it. But here in the deep deep South in the dreamy mud of the riverbend at New Orleans, we do know it. It's only a change in the light, a knifeblade-thin change from bright white to reddish. It's only a sweat drop's difference in dryness, enough to bring glad news to skin resigned to endless discomfort. It's only a sudden spurt of a playful breeze, coming in on top of a river wavelet all the way from Cairo, Illinois. It's also those signs devised by humans to signal the turning of the year: the corner drugstore full of nice-smelling new school supplies and swarms of kids in crisp uniforms chattering at the bus stop. There is a surge of buoyancy, or maybe just a reflex, in the manner, if not the result, of somnolent bureaucrats in city offices. Elsewhere in the country, where the efficient Americans live, offices are crackling with energy. The phones are ringing, tans are admired, files fly. Here, we get only a degree of such admirable action. Still, it's enough to know that autumn is here. Your cornucopia is our shadow of a smile. It is said that all of America's work is done between Labor Day and Thanksgiving. It's a wonder we are still such a productive country. Other places must be much like New Orleans, where we wallow in saints and feasts and festivals and are continually amazed by the steaming of the earth and the wild proliferation of life. We work only at recognizing the awesomeness of the universe, which is a job, too. People else-where produce. We exult, admire, celebrate, reproduce. And now is such a time, though it's only a hint. In the subtle gradation of light, which to the coarse senses would seem no more than a flicker, we find a plethora of stun-ning revelations. Makes you want to dance. Or at least begin thinking of the autumn balls, and this year's masque.

Air Travel and
the Advance of Demonism

I flew on ValueJet from New Orleans to Atlanta the day the Atlanta-bound Valuejet from Florida crashed. I found no great difference be-tween ValueJet's service or Delta's or American's. In fact, I preferred the breezy style of the ValueJet staff to the cranky institutional style of Ameri-can. The sad truth is that air travel has gotten worse in every respect in the last few years. Mechanical problems are a routine occurrence that causes endless delays for which no one apologizes anymore. My Delta flight from San Francisco to Dallas left an hour late for unexplained reasons, which made several of us miss our connection by a mere five minutes. In the old days, the connecting flight would have waited. But this isn't the old days when there was some class to flying. Courtesy and concern are gone. So is food. There is nothing but lousy peanuts and pretzels for hours and even those are severely rationed as if the nation were at war. I saw a starving kid reach for some extra peanuts and the steward shot right on by like he was carrying the corporate caviar stash. Gone too is any semblance of comfort: The seats get smaller and smaller as American butts get bigger and bigger. Coach class now resembles steerage on the nineteenth-century ships that brought immigrants to America. Everybody's jammed in like sardines and expected, doubtlessly, to break out in songs of gratitude for being ferried to Atlanta. I will have to be excused, though, from breaking out into a Delta hymn while an overfed salesman is mashing me with his hams. Gone too is cleanliness. Harried ground crews now give planes a quick going over in the minutes between flights. They are gone in a flash, leaving old sandwich wrappers and crumpled newspapers wedged in the seats. And you are lucky if that's all you find wedged in there. I wear gloves when I fly now. Oh, by the way, ValueJet specialized in bad jokes. On our way to Atlanta we were asked to add up our birth month, date, and shoe size. The lowest and highest number would get prizes. The guy in front of me was born 12/31 and was shoe size 11. He won something in a plastic bag. That was, recognizably, a joke. On other airlines they don't need to tell jokes. They *are* jokes.

Note: The devil-automobile is responsible for what the poet Lawrence Ferlinghetti calls "autogeddon." The devil-airplane is responsible for, among other things, cultural defilement (by taking certain people to places where they were never meant to be), loss of feeling for the true and awesome dimensions of the country, and angel impersonation.

Berkeley

A friend of mine invited me to his birthday party in a bar in the Republic of Berkeley. It was one of those fog-chilled California evenings when the cold knifes you for no good reason and you stand there shivering but certain that it could never get THIS cold in California. And then you comfort yourself with the thought that at least it doesn't get any *colder*. And then it does. Anyway, I opened the door of the bar ignoring the homeless person who tried to sell me the homeless newspaper. I already had five of them and they were all about two months old: I guess time is slower when you're homeless.

The bar was well lit, cozy, crowded and warm. On stage, a gang of Che Guevaras, or five kids with Che berets, were wailing nostalgically something about "the revolution." Which one, I wondered. I soon found out. I barely recognized my friends when I spotted them. I hadn't seen them in about ten years and they had grown old. Old! Their hair was white, their noses were bigger, their flesh hung sadly about once-sturdy bones. I shouted out François Villon's verse, "Old age, you fierce pig!" even as I hugged them. I was so rattled by this sight I lit a cigarette. All of a sudden, from every corner of the bar, young men and women who looked like younger versions of us, only with more hair and tauter flesh, started screaming at me: "There is no smoking here!" I understood now what "revolution" the Ches on stage were wailing about: It was the revolution of young conformists against the old nonconformists—us. I dragged my friends outside for a smoke and, although they didn't smoke, they all lit a silent cigarette in solidarity against the righteous young. A ridiculous vehicle shaped like a brioche whooshed by with barely any sound, like a snake slithering off a rock. "What was THAT?" I exclaimed, frightened. My friends explained that it was an electric car. It was silent, it could be plugged in for a charge at the BART station, it was ecologically beneficial, and it could run you down like a bug even at its maximum speed of thirty-five miles per hour because you couldn't hear it coming. And that was just like old age: natural, slow, and you can't hear it coming. The "revolution," I realized, consisted of just one boring, old refrain: "You are old and we are young. We are healthy and you're sick." I bought another paper from the homeless guy: ALL the news is old.

ψ

Ratio of Derriere versus Frontal

The Supreme Court let stand an anti–nude dancing ruling by a lower court in Florida after arguments in which it took 346 words to define a derriere and 69 to describe the female frontal region. In other words, there are roughly four times as many words for the back-o-zone, a ratio that seems exaggerated on the face of it. Granted, the derriere may at most be twice as large as the front. But there are surely numerous cases where the derriere is only half the size of the front. Granted also that both females and males sport a more or less identical behind, so that it's possible more words were coined over time by both sexes. Clearly, the derriere is the better known of the two and subject to a great deal more attention in both the vulgate and the savantic. The derriere also has three extra functions, namely waste elimination, seating support, and use in insults, which feed their own vocabularies into the region. However, in terms of visibility , both derriere and breasts are out there, unlike the genital regions which are buried in mystery and, doubtlessly, inarticulation.

Anthropologists have theorized that when our species rose upright female genitalia became folded in and hidden while the male's became exposed and vulnerable. The derriere and female breasts, on the other hand, became more pronounced in both sexes. And if that is the case, why is the derriere getting away with all the words? Is it because it's funnier? In Germany, for instance, the derriere is considered so funny that its mere mention causes waves of hilarity. It is a pity that the Supreme Court heard no arguments about the rest of our naughty parts. It is my guess that the number of terms used to describe breasts, 69, may be identical to that of terms regarding other male and female characteristics. If that is the case, and why shouldn't it be, both the numbers of male and female terms together, the sum of everything we hide, would still pale before the derriere. The law now, as it stands in St. John's County, Florida, requires that one-third of a dancer's buttocks must be covered and about one-fourth of females' breasts. Those Supreme Court judges, seated firmly on their derrieres, ought to have pondered the paucity of terms before jumping to their conclusion. Instead of forbidding nude dancing, they should have required it until the frontal vocabulary reached parity with the behindal.

Beauty & Safety

Whenever I go to a beautiful place, I imagine myself living there. I went to Boone, North Carolina, a mountain-sheltered paradise where rustic craftsmen sell quilts from shops that smell like pine. On the way there, Moravian cookie makers in sixteenth-century clothes sell you paper-thin ginger wafers. They bake them in the huge ovens that scared the daylights out of Hansel and Gretel. What is it with paradise that inspires instant terror? I asked Lynn Doyle, local poet and observer, after we bought these great cookies. I don't know, Lynn said, all I know is that Boone, North Carolina, is at the center of international intrigue. You won't get too far running over here. Lynn informed me that just a short time before I arrived, a Swede was found murdered in the woods. This Swede, it turns out, had once been suspected in the assassination of Sweden's prime minister. It was speculated that other assassin Swedes might be hiding in these beautiful mountains. But the intrigue suffered when it was discovered that a local sherif's deputy probably killed the Swede for visiting his girlfriend's trailer on the full moon. And not long before that, said Lynn, two fighter jets cornered a single-engine dope plane all the way from Mexico to near Boone and caused it to crash. No one was thought to have survived this crash, but a day or so later two really beat-up guys were hitchhiking up the road. They were picked up and never seen again. You mean they got away?

I gasped. Sure did, said Lynn, with that look of, "we sure don't like the feds around here." There must still be gin mills up here, I said in wonder. Sure are, replied Lynn. Later I met a man with a wild beard named Tommy Thompson who told me that when I got a motorcycle I should come to his place, a bed & breakfast for bikers. I think I will. Get a bike, that is. Have Budweiser for breakfast. Roar into the clouds pouring in between the peaks of the Blue Ridge Mountains.

Part Six

Virtuality Takes

Command

Virtuality Takes Command

Thank you for asking me here to speak in person. It's so retro. You could have easily produced a virtual Codrescu to do the job—and in a few years, I am sure, the virtual Codrescu will be as close to the real thing as a set of parameters can produce.

You can still experience me virtually, however, if you close your eyes. It will be just like listening to the radio.

But I doubt that any of you are interested in virtuality to that extent. In fact, you'll have to look hard to find anyone—and that includes the techno-geeks at Microsoft—who is so invested in virtuality that he would prefer to get his information without the ambiguous and paradoxical participation of all the senses.

It would be hard indeed to find such a person, but there are some who come close. I met two young men who spend over fourteen hours a day in something called MUD—a Multiuser Dungeon—which is an imaginary world created by a number of players with shifting and evolving identities, many of whom are part human and part animals. These two cybernauts kept their eyes to the ground while I spoke to them, and when I asked them if they felt uncomfortable in human society, they both nodded yes. When I pressed them about what exactly made them uncomfortable, one of them mumbled, "It's limited."

That surprised me because I would have thought that the opposite might have been the case. Spending fourteen hours glued to the screen, using very little of your body, seems limited to *me*. I am no great sportsman, but I get tremendous enjoyment from the pure animal activity of a body which, I believe, puts forth its own information and discovers things that are not immediately quantifiable.

But then it turned out that these two guys were pursuing an interdisciplinary, cross-species Ph.D. in Cultural Studies. They were post-humanists.

And as far as I could see, they had all the elements that would make for a successful academic career later on. They were utterly dependent on a machine that, like the university, provided for their physical needs; they had an ideology that was virtually defiant but only virtually so; they could question and change identity at the push of a button; and they related to other entities that shared their ideology. They could push the limits, any limits, including biological ones; they could include all the excluded they could imagine; they transgressed cultural and social borders; they were interdisciplinary, nomadic, and free-spirited, all within the sixteen-inch dimensions of their fishbowl. And they barely had time to eat, sleep, or read books.

Most of the computer folk I've talked to in Seattle tell me that they spend an average of ten to fourteen hours in cyberspace. The eight-hour workday no longer exists for most Americans plugged into a computer. My friend Linda Stone designs virtual reality environments, which she studies for clues to emerging behaviors in cyberspace. Her own code of ethics forbids her to interact in cyberspace under any persona too radically different from her own, which is represented by an Avatar. Linda's ethics are unusual in cyberspace—most VR users are postmodernists, who are there precisely in order to get away from their habitual definition. Or, as the Czech writer Robert Gal put it, "My moral code prevents me from being myself."

Linda designed her Avatar with an eye to accurate self-representation: It was a cartoon of a bespectacled young woman dressed in a business suit. I didn't point out that the Avatar was slimmer and crisper somehow, and that it would stay that way throughout its cyber-interactions, while she, herself, might look less than crisp after fourteen hours at her computer terminal. The one nagging problem of virtuality right now is that a physical being persists in being singularly present both before and after the virtual experiment. I expect that this won't be a problem for long.

Anyone can design their own Avatar, as well as select one from a preexisting menu of various types, depending on what environment one chooses to haunt. The one we visited was a bar called Cheers, which was fairly G-rated, and the Avatar menu offered a Popeye the Sailor, a Vixen, a Cigar-Chomping Financier, a Dandy, a Torch Singer, and I forget what else. These beings communicated through cartoon balloons over their heads that filled with words when you typed. It was possible also to conduct a private conversation with only one other person: In that case, the words appeared in a balloon circumscribed by a dotted—instead of an unbroken—line.

Behavior in cyberspace was soon demonstrated in two ways: A Torch Singer said, apropos of nothing, to the five or six people in the room: "My boyfriend is gay. Any advice?," to which a Vixen replied, "I am really a gay man. What do you want to know?" At the same time, Popeye approached Linda and said, "Whatcha doing Friday night?" Linda clicked on Popeye's profile and discovered that Popeye was a soldier stationed in Bosnia. She replied privately, "What's Bosnia like?" Surprise. "How did you know?" While Linda and the soldier became involved in a private conversation, the group was discussing the dilemma of the woman with the gay boyfriend. Floating in the distance at the far end of the bar were two arches resembling McDonald's. "What's there?" I asked. "That," Linda said, "is the portal to another world."

All of these encounters in all their complexity were taking place in real time. The line dividing the virtual and the real was extremely blurred: After a while I fell into Linda's habit of dropping the word "virtual," and describing what was happening inside the screen in the same terms as our interaction outside the screen. And, in fact, there was little distinction. We were barely conscious of any border between the inside and the outside: We were utterly involved in the exchange. The only difference was that if we got bored we could escape to another world, or to another university, one less connected to possibly real problems in this here—possibly—real world.

In Seattle, where Linda works, I met a number of cyberspace luminaries. I met two game designers who had worked for the U.S. military and were now turning their attention to the commercial market. They strapped me into a headset and I headed down a tunnel where various entities were shooting at me. Or so I thought, until they told me that it was I who was shooting the entities—but being part of "the old paradigm," I couldn't tell who was me in cyberspace. I was identifying with the enemy. Since I wasn't going to die anyway, I had a hard time figuring out why the enemy was the enemy, though I would have known it instinctively had I been a true cyber-naut.

I met a medical researcher who designs training environments for doctors. I killed a perfectly good virtual patient by following a heart-surgery map. This environment was doubtessly useful, just like air-flight simulators are useful, but it was a scientific, not a cultural, environment.

I also met Dr. Brickman, one of the founders of VR, now working on the next generation of virtuality-generating systems. Dr. Brickman found both the Internet and VR in its present form quaintly passé. The next step was complete virtuality, technology capable of creating complete sensorial immersion. I got the impression that the meshing of biological and cybernetic systems was not far off, and that defining "human beings" was going to become a lot more difficult in the near future.

You may well ask, what *really* does any of this have to do with us? I wouldn't blame you if you did. Some people may see the coming virtuality as simply an opportunity to create better research and learning opportunities with the aid of clever programming. Already, many of us are becoming quite adept at using the Internet and learning the idioms of interactivity to become more efficient.

But more efficient at *what*? Already there are cars that can whisk us away from campus at a moment's notice, television sets to calm our agitated minds, advertising to incorporate us in the larger community, consumption needs that involve some serious forays into capitalism, personal relationships that need therapy and drugs, and labor issues having to do with pay raises needed to keep all the above functioning. Does cyberspace provide a support system for the bothersome difficulties of making a nice bourgeois academic living while deconstructing the society that makes it impossible?

And I didn't even mention students who are truly lost in cyberspace, hoping to meet us there for an all-too-brief virtual confrontation—that they are going to win. In cyberspace. Virtually.

I am surely exaggerating, but I would like to know, for instance, how the make-believe world of cyberspace participates in our efforts to understand a century in which human beings have done their practical best to eliminate humans altogether. For one thing, to answer my own question, we have more information. We have records on film and tape of the testimonies of Holocaust survivors, for instance. We have tons of information that needs only the authority of a compassionate analysis to yield a moral charge. But I challenge you to find a minibyte of such compassionate authority for every million megabytes of information. The "author" with the authority to produce such a moral charge has been dismantled by various ideologies. It is amazing to see that, fifty years since the Holocaust, and one decade since the prolapse of communism, ideologies and not moral outrage are still the dominant trend in our cultural, virtual, never-never lands.

That's not our job, some of you may be thinking. We are not preachers, demagogues, prophets, or Steven Spielberg. We are scholars whose job is to work with text, produce text, and provide whatever textual interpretations we think are viable. In this respect, most of us see the new technology as something we can use in support of textuality, a sort of "visual aids," as the old phrase quaintly had it.

But when our students are wearing computers capable of keeping them involved in several environments at once, we might have to accept the fact that we are just one "channel" in a menu offering thousands. If you think that it's difficult now to know where a daydreaming student is, you can imagine the problem of locating the missing student traveling virtually through designed environments whose sole purpose is to tune out text.

Daydreaming has already been replaced to a large extent by programming. Television has effectively turned daydreamers into screenwriters—and when I say that the purpose of programming is to tune out text I mean precisely that. We may have to resign ourselves to becoming "textual aids" to an interactive, visual world.

What this interactive, visual world says—what its text is—is made infinitely more complex, however, by the fact that this text does not give a fig for interpretation, or criticism.

The longer we live in the Age of the Image, the more we are rewired into an eternal present. In the future, there will be plenty of text, of course, but text to be looked at, visually. A "text" will always be present, but it will be only one of many graphic devices with a fading referential universe. This referential universe will be crowded in by images that will replace psychological, social, moral, and religious narratives, while strengthening political manipulation. Or just manipulation. The basic text of the coming virtuality will be "The User's Guide," which, with appended "Operating Instructions," will replace the Constitution, the Bible, and all our books. It will be written in a language not subject to multiple interpretations—hopefully—and blindingly clear to the user, or the addict. No one will ever know that the ancestor of this language was none other than the Pidgin English that once came with cheap transistor radios made in Hong Kong, a mysterious language that itself succeeded the Ur-language of the Mechanical Age known as "Instructions-for-Assembly."

Politics in the age of the image is almost entirely virtual. I say "almost," because now and then the body politic surprises itself by going directly to the source, to television, for its inspiration, bypassing entirely the conventional paid political imagery—as was the case when Minnesotans elected Jesse "the Body" Ventura governor. Jesse was more "organic TV" than paid political advertising TV. Such a politics is "ultra virtual."

Within the virtuality of national politics resides the secondary virtuality of academic politics which, being textual, harks back to the quaint (textual) notions of Left and Right.

The right would like to preserve an idealized memory in order to prevent too many "outsiders," from changing the so-called canon. The left would like to begin in an idealized all-inclusive future and proceed backward to revise the right's idealized history. In the ideological rush to define what kind of democracy we should have, we have been ignoring certain factors that make such discussion tenuous if not downright moot.

In the first place, American society has been changing at a pace that our cultural critics haven't even begun to map, let alone comprehend. By the next decade, Spanish will be spoken as much as English. New waves of immigrants are altering the physical space of cities, confounding old patterns of behavior, diet, and community. Electoral patterns are changing, as more and more outsider groups find their political voice. Books by new Americans are appearing at a staggering rate. There is a flourishing poetry scene in the big cities, where new languages, such as Nuyorican, can be heard. Music, theater, and art, are acquiring accents, new textures, tastes, and moves. What Gomez-Pena, the Chicano performance artist, calls Border World is a whole new culture on both sides of the Mexican-American border.

At the same time, resistance to these changes has been growing and organizing. We are seeing the rise of fascist militias in every state of the Union. The Christian right had the electoral savvy to direct a whole Republican Revolution. Goodbye, Mr. Gingrich—we won't miss you. Nationalist movements based on race can provoke millions to direct action.

These phenomena confound pristine notions of Left and Right. The militias espouse quite a bit of the populism that used to be part of leftist jargon not long ago. The Christian right learned networking and resistance techniques from the old left. A new black political class has turned sixties idealism into nineties cynicism without changing a syllable of the old rhetoric. Politically correct legislation of sexuality in the workplace lies in tatters in the aftermath of a dose of presidential reality. In academia, never mind Right or Left, the battle wages incessantly over self-preservation and self-promotion. This is a game of make-believe in which ideological directions are invoked solely for the purpose of giving some sorely needed dignity to the endless struggle for crumbs. There is certainly a market here for a Virtual game that could train academics for the Battle of the Hallways the way pilots train for flight in a simulated environment. It would feature the "as-if book," a book intended not to be read but to become a line in a résumé.

Language and reality are at odds almost everywhere you look, from legislation to cultural criticism. In this gap between language and reality, television and cyberspace flourish. The image factories care for neither memory nor visionary revisionism. In the realm of the Image all is postmodernly equal. Politics is now the art of manipulating images that are impervious to textual criticism. A politics without memory tends to become authoritarianism, or as is the case now, corporatism. A politics without vision tends toward the same result. Interactivity and networking may help circulate ideas in a certain kind of defense against visual propaganda, but the very medium they are employing renders them ineffective. Marshall McLuhan was so right. The medium *is* the message.

We are witnessing the mingling of public and private, mingled and mixed according to the way images mix, timelessly, seamlessly, without translation or the necessity for translation. Images bypass the critical locus through which words traditionally pass. Neither time nor analysis nor contemplation nor translation stand between our direct perception of this metamorphing spectacle. There is no longer any "inside," whether the "inner self" or "inside information," there is in fact no longer any distinction between the inside and outside, or between the private and the public.

Meanwhile, the reality of our democracy pushes on, wildly, untranslated, waxing and waning in confrontations that are very serious, yet barely rate the attention of our cultural critics, trapped between old ideas of Left and Right, or bogged down in theoretical mumbo jumbo.

How did we get here?

What was once, not very long ago in narrative time, an artistic hope has proven to be only an alarm signal, the cry of the canary in the mine. There was a hope, in the heady days of the late fifties and mid-sixties, that the image might lead an autonomous but neighbor-friendly life with critical thought. There was, for instance, the matter of abstract painting, which was presented as a modality of thinking in process, thinking deconditioning itself, untranslating itself. The end product, never very important to the artistic activity, was an image that invited activity more than contemplation, an activity that presupposed wresting some freedom from increasingly oppressive contexts, including translation. This is still a commendable, though hardly possible, utopia. It is the equivalent of taking a vacation, which is only a dream in the intensely confrontational time crisis of the fin-de-millennium.

What Gilles deLeuze calls "the powers of the false" can no longer be divided, as deLeuze does, into the "organic" and the "crystalline," or images that stand in for a preexistent reality—the organic—and those that "constitute their own object," referring to "purely optical and sound situations detached from their motor extensions."* The organic image presupposes a narrative bridge between the real and the imaginary, while the crystalline subverts this narrative because it "replaces the object, both creates and erases it." The crystalline image, and deLeuze quotes Robbe-Grillet here, is the cinema "of the seer and no longer of the agent (*de voyant, non plus d'actant*)."

This avant-garde cinema, along with abstract painting and other ambitions of decontextualization, have been buried under the debris of their own products. The speed with which even the purest squiggle is commodified testifies to the triumph of the image principally in the elimination of the necessity for translation. In other words, not only do images not need translation (which wasn't always the case) but they always speak *in translation*. The original of this translation, which is the creative act, resolves itself in the secondary language. I say that this wasn't always the case because the image, until television and advertising, was an object of contemplation that demanded translation.

Virtuality is television squared. The interactivity that would seem to distinguish it from the unidirectional flow of television takes place on *the other side of the screen*, inside television itself. We have literally stepped inside the

---

*Gilles Deleuze, *Cinema 2: The Time Image* (Minneapolis: Minnesota University Press, 1986), 126.

little screen to play by the rules of the little people in there. The passivity of the TV watcher now seems like a form of freedom, compared to the compulsory activity of the cybernaut.

The Internet right now appears to be a kind of crack in the Empire of the Image. The Internet is still, by and large, textual, and even images follow language in this first of what will certainly be many forms of Internet. The Internet, at present, stands in relation to the image exactly where language stood in relation to the image in, let's say, 1914, when the Dada movement first exploded the narratives of the previous century.

But the Internet is only virtually textual, image-disguised-as-text. The virtuality will become more apparent as the medium becomes more sophisticated. It would be unwise to consider the current text-based Internet as anything more than a primitive model. On the one hand, everyone is thrilled by its utopian promise; on the other, it insidiously extorts our time and energy.

What exactly are we doing in cyberspace? Well, one thing we are doing, besides reading and writing e-mail to and from people with offices next door, is surrendering the awkwardness of the body and in so doing, perfecting ourselves. Even better, we are insulating against any confrontations with reality by building our own little personality cults. These are called personal Web pages. Each one of these Web pages is a miniature personality cult, literally, if we look at the scale of, let's say, Stalin's personality cult, which was writ large on billboards and mountainsides. Seeking perfection through a mini–personality cult testifies to the continuing siren song of utopia, which is to say, the persistence of ideologies.

Like most people, I am of two minds about the Internet, though you may not think so after all I've said. One of my minds is thrilled, despite my better sense, by its utopian promise. The other mind, thank God—again—is resolutely skeptical. My utopian streak is personal and generational. I came of age in the sixties, and optimism is our generational disease. We believed that the world was going to get better through our efforts and, some might argue, it has. It has certainly gotten wilder, and it is both amusing and horrifying to see how some of our baby ideas grew up.

The skeptical mind is equally stubborn. I grew up in communist Romania, where the promises and language of utopia were used to create hell on earth. This mind cautions that utopianism is only a clever form of hypnosis whose real work is the extortion of energy from human beings. In the name of utopian sentiment we can be made to sacrifice our liberties and, in the end, our bodies. This mind is suspicious of rationality, of abstraction, of anything that calls for going against one's self-interest. This mind is against the deferral of pleasure for the sake of some future goal, and it defends the perimeters of the physical body as fiercely as any animal defending its territory.

These two minds are irreconcilable though they clearly coexist.

The Christian philosopher Teilhard de Chardin posited in the 1940s the idea of a spiritual-affective atmosphere he called "the noosphere," which surrounded the planet just like the atmosphere. Within the noosphere, our thoughts, feelings, and yearnings linked up with everybody else's in a continual thickening of substance. This was a kind of lowering of the heavens into earthly existence, an ombudsman afterlife, or, if you are Catholic, a purgatory. The development of this spirit-world-within-matter was necessitated by an increasing evolutionary pressure within us to join in the process of creation, or the "evolving Christ" as Teilhard de Chardin called it.

The noosphere is now somewhat perceptible through the pedestrian tools of access to the Internet, which is a rudimentary representation of this afterlife. The Internet as it exists now is only potentially "noospheric," because it still consists mainly of raw information unfolding within a partial global conversation. The voices within this exchange belong to the world's affluent minority. Eventually though, utopists tell us, everybody will be participating. When this happens, we will be living simultaneously on earth and in spirit.

The afterlife accessible through technology will make life more sprpiritual for everybody, creating, in effect, a utopian community. This community will see to any number of our material needs, but it will also ensure a kind of immortality in virtual space (virtual beings don't die) and an access to other, potential levels hitherto denied mere mortals.

It's a pretty picture, but let's look at the cost. In the first place, the advent of cyberspace will necessitate the abandonment of the physical body. In exchange, we will acquire a virtual body that can be as sensate, or even more richly sensate, than our current body. Virtuality can enhance the senses, without the psychological complexity of real sensual enhancement. You can have guilt-free orgasms with any other virtual beings, just as you can experience the peaks of the Himalayas without dying on the ice.

However, virtuality is rational, and herein lies its horror. The virtual body is designed by mathematics and, no matter how seemingly lifelike the design is, it cannot replicate the workings of the mysterious complexity of life. Reality demands both pain and failure: Success can only have substance in this context. An organism cannot be called "successful" solely through design. Life needs adventure, it is predicated on the irrational urge to journey physically toward danger. No simulation or virtuality will work here because their outcomes are predictable. Nobody will accept a utopia that contains the possibility of pain.

Cyberspace is hypnotic, a quality inherent in other media, such as television and advertising. We have long ago ceased to think critically about television, no matter the whining of pundits. Television bypasses critical sense, it speaks directly to the emotional vortex in one's stomach. Advertising is, likewise, a medium for which we have no defenses: it speaks directly to the human desire to be comforted and transformed within the cultural norm. Both those media are firmly in control of that infinite desiring mechanism that can be quenched only by having more. Addiction, in short. "User's manual," indeed. Cyberspace adds a new twist to the addictive power of those media by creating the illusion of a dialogue between addictions that can pass for free will. The actual content of cyberspace now is a combination of image banks and shopping opportunities disguised as information and dialogue. The data banks are display windows: The information is free but possessing it sets in motion the urge to shop its source, or its meta-content. Internet dialogue is directed either toward sex (shopping "the body without organs") or toward networking product-development.

Still, there may be nothing wrong with the infinite (infinitely depressing to me) cycle of consumption-production, if it produces more wealth and makes more people happy. This wealth does, however, come from somewhere: namely from the physical energy of the people wired into cyberspace. The fact that Americans watch eight hours of television a day is now being superseded by those other Americans I mentioned who spend twelve to fourteen hours in cyberspace every day. These new cyber-beings do not need communal spaces (cities, schools, or churches), sweaty relationships to physical beings, nature, or animals. *They need nothing from the outside.* An absolute interiority has taken command of them. In exchange for their sacrifice of the outside, they have gained a sensory paradise, a virtual existence and afterlife.

This utopia starts to look more and more like the communist utopia: an upper-class gulag. There are no barbed-wire fences, but the outside is just as resolutely out of reach. The question is, in the end, ecological: What is the effect of a designed afterlife on a physical planet? Can it sustain virtuality, or the disappearance of humans into cyberspace, or does it become an uncontested source for the raw materials needed to keep the cyber-trippers happy? What do the animals have to say about it?

The notion of what a "human being" is has undergone some severe jolts for over a century now, and there are few agreements on the matter. Most of us agree that it is some kind of "construct," but what exactly has been and is still constructing it is a matter of debate. There are those among us who think that life is but a joke—sorry, Bob Dylan just blew into my head— there are some among us who think that there is no such thing as a human being at all, that all of it, humans, nature, and technology, are under construction, and that only relations of power—or access to construction materials—are worth our (post) humanist attention. A human being is *already* virtual: The projection of whatever pulls her strings. But whatever it is or isn't, *it* is not finished—which is why we (and various its) keep working.

There is no disagreement on this: Human beings are unfinished. Theologians and Marxists can shake hands on this one. God has a plan, Marx had a plan. Those plans are called utopia: only *there* will human beings be completely finished. God's garden needs a lot of weeding and Marx's utopia proved to be Wal-Mart, but never mind: The utopian urge is there and it isn't going away.

The new virtuality is a competitor. It competes not only with reality, that old virtuality, but with all those other utopias, as well.

Reality is scary. Rendering it innocuous underlies most of the contracts we keep trying to honor but which we did not write. Rendering reality unconscious is the job of most social virtuality—which works for Bill Gates.

And then there are those among us—among whom I once found myself—who find virtuality satisfying because it seemingly multiplies and transforms identity to the limits of one's imagination. This was once a poetic desideratum: Human beings are so loathsome, splitting them up might make them less harmful. I think of Fernando Pessoa's "heteronyms," for instance, or my own invented personae in early poems, and find them now— like abstract painting and underground cinema—only awkward forerunners of the huge industry of the imagination.

The constant calls for "creativity" and "content" now issuing from the ever-hungry maws of the new media are nothing less than calls for the drafting of our entire society for the purposes of writing poetry or, if you prefer, formatting what's left of reality, for broadcast.

Siegfried Gideon, in his classic book *Mechanization Takes Command*, described the gradual conquest of the world by mechanization and foresaw the abrupt end of the mechanical age. We can see that the virtual is taking command, but it's hard to foresee what lies beyond its imagined infinity.

There are also young people who like to use technology to an opposite means: to enhance the senses, to exacerbate physicality, to provoke whatever is most human and untechnological in themselves. To *imagine* as little as possible. Techno-raves and Ecstasy are two of these aids to superphysicality. What is *their* politics?

Which brings me back the two MUDders I met in Seattle. The existence of the outside world scared them. And for good reason. At the world's largest shopping mall in Minneapolis—the Mall of America—I saw two other cultural studies scholars strapped into Virtual Reality gear. These two pudgy cybernauts had an amazing array of expressions on their faces as they dodged dangers, fought evil, and generally triumphed in heroic fashion over untold programming. Watching them at a distance of about two feet were three tough-looking Chicano hombres wearing gang colors and grinning like bobcats who'd come across two captive turkeys.

That scene gave me great hope—thank god for the barbarians. We do miss the barbarians, don't we? Cavafy had it so right: "Now what's going to happen to us without the barbarians? / They were, those people, a kind of solution."*

---

*Edmund Keeley and Philip Sherrard, trans., *Cavafy*.

The V-Chip

Why bother putting the V-chip in everyone's TV when you can put it directly into everybody's brain? It would be like a flu shot and afterward you'll never want to watch violence or sex again, you'll be going to church every Sunday and always looking on the sunny side of life. You'll be nice all day long and at night you'll sleep unless it's the time of the year when you must procreate. In fact, the V-chip could be programmed to get TV direct into the brain so you won't need a TV set anymore. The nice, violence- and sex-free shows will just pour in behind your eyebrows and entertain you from within. And the commercials won't even bother you because they'll go directly to your money and make you spend while you watch. No need to move at all. You can even vote out of the V-chip by just wiggling your toes, once for the Democrats, twice for the Republicans. The V-chip, which by now is an E or Everything-Chip, can also contain health information that will keep your cholesterol and blood pressure in check so that you can live forever and do as much good as you can while consuming as much as possible without any ill effects. And there will be a timer to remind you that it's time to put on deodorant. When your chip gets old you can choose to have it replaced or you can just fade away with the chipless masses of the Third World. The chipless people of the world will die sweaty in sinful cities by their hobo fires. These cities, full of temptation and outlaws who've ripped the chip out of their heads, will eventually have to be eradicated. By contrast, the eternal suburb of the chip people will be just like heaven, all harp music and singing puppy dogs and malls as soft as a pillow, void of pain and art. All the cravings for violence and sex that the media woke in us will be collected for the government by private storage companies who will scrape them off your V-chips every month or so. They will be stored in big pools of a new strategic reserve to be released by the army if a new Hitler or something shows up. Thank you for the V-chip, Mr. President. Tomorrow will definitely be another day.

AOL Addict Tells All

S lowly, slowly, without thinking, I've become addicted to America Online. There is only a difference of degree between AOL and all the
other faceless corporations I'm addicted to, like AT&T, BellSouth, or
Entergy. The difference is important, though: I submit blindly to those corporations because they provide what I think are "essential services." Things
like AOL are luxuries on their way to becoming "essential services." When
you are fully addicted to e-mail, you can bet it's an essential service. There
was a time when electricity and telephone service were luxuries too, but
they quickly became indispensable. In fact, there is very little that now
presses down ubiquitously on our fin-de-millennium heads that is truly and
completely indispensible. It's only that we are junkies, we can't do without
them.

For the most part, our providers of "essential services" function invisibly,
like the gods, as long as they get their monthly sacrifices, but now and then
one of these gods malfunctions or it freaks and then you find yourself in hell.
In Voice Mail Hell. Trying to reach a human being on the telephone you
have to wander for years in the electronic desert, and when you do you
might as well speak to a machine. People in Voice Mail Hell have only first
names and no fixed location. They could be next door or they could be in
Alaska. In addition to having no idea who or where this person is, you can-

not even be sure what corporation this person works for. The name of a company tells you nothing about who owns it, what it does, what nation it considers home. The modern corp is a multi-tentacled organism, a rhizomatous creature without a center, or in English, an infinite potato. You can cut off one branch and the organism feels nothing. It sprouts another branch somewhere else. BancOne has recently sprouted hundreds of branch offices all over Louisiana, some of them located in buildings owned by banks that were swallowed overnight by BancOne. All of these branches are equal, they are commanded from some remote space reachable only by years of wandering in Cyber or Voice Mail Hell.

AOL is a gateway to cyberspace, they bill the gates, so to speak, and, after you become used to it, you go through those gates fearlessly, as if they were the gates to your own house. Of course, you don't have to pay when you pass through the gates of your own house, or I hope you don't. Over the gates of your own house there is no inscription, or if there is, it's usually your name or something friendly like Villa Maris. The gates of AOL are more like the gates of hell, over which it says, "Abandon all hope, ye who enter here." And you do, abandon hope, that is, because you just wanna have cyber-fun.

I have accepted all of this with weary resignation. So when my address book disintegrated in AOL, I wanted to believe that it was an accident. I got a brand-new AOL program and I started all over again, calling all my friends and re-creating my address book. No sooner was I done than the address book self-destroyed again. This time, I suspected something structurally wrong in the very gut of the giant. The address book is vital: It is where you keep all your friends' cyber-addresses and where you go when you write someone. Losing your address book is tragic, it makes you feel alone in the world, just a flesh critter with no cyber-friends. It's an emergency.

I called AOL and wandered through Voice Mail Hell until Karl answered. He admitted that there had been a lot of calls about destroyed address books.

"What happened?" I cried out in despair.

"It corrupted," said Karl sternly, as if that "it" had somehow been my fault.

"What do you mean 'it'? It must be some flaw in AOL!"

Karl's voice really hardened now: "There is no flaw in AOL!" he answered officially, "It just corrupted, that's all. You have to destroy it and start over."

I was sure now that Karl had something to hide. "What's your full name, Karl?"

"I don't have to give you my full name," said AOL Karl.

"Where are you, Karl?"

"I cannot tell you this."

"How does the AOL address book become corrupted?"

Karl hung up. The awful silence of Voice Mail Hell closed in on all sides.

I anxiously opened my program. It functioned. AOL had not (yet) avenged itself by cutting off my supply. I could live without my address book. I will make one on paper. And when they decide to destroy all my saved mail, I won't complain. Nor will I make much noise when they tell me how to vote. Or what to buy. Or when to eat. I can't. I need access. It's sad, but it's a done deal. I just wish they would all merge into a single entity, Bell-South, BancOne, AOL, Entergy, the whole evil overlord pantheon. That way, at least, we would all know that we are subjects of the Generic Company of America and would feel a lot less anxious. Bill the gates, but make it all one bill. That kind of merger is how the last monotheism got its start.

The Mouse with Glowing Ears

N ow that the mouse with glowing ears has arrived, the fashion body will become reality. Forget all those piercings and tattoos—they only skimmed the surface. Now we can put firefly genes to work to make us glow-in-the dark fingers and belly buttons. We can put wolf genes to work to give us a bristle of wolf-hair down our backs. We can grow splendid lemur tails and, best of all, we can fulfill humanity's age-old dream: wings. Yes, a pair of sturdy owl wings planted firmly in our shoulder blades could lift us at long last from the skin of the earth and into the blue. Genetics has opened a way both into the past and into the future: We can now mix again with animals just like the Greek gods mixed with humans, but we won't have to do it the old-fashioned way by grabbing the beasts by their necks and subduing them. The minotaur and the demigod will line up for anesthesia not rumbling. Romulus and Remus can once more suckle their wolf-mother while shepherd boys can again regale their favorite sheep with their stories, because while their favorite sheep will look for all purposes like sheep, they will in fact be humans in sheep's bodies. Movie stars will grow their own fur coats with the help of mink genes, making the killing of minks unnecessary, and the fury of antifur activists moot. Of course, these movie stars will have to wear their furs all the time because gene mixes are permanent; they will have to live in Alaska where a permanent fur coat is good.

While Hollywood will surely move to Alaska, other parts of the U.S. will serve different gene mixes: Winged people will all live along the Continental Divide in order to better swoop down from peaks over valleys. Glowing people will live in New York and other tunneled, wormy metropolises. Wolf geners will dwell in the pack zones of the North. Insect-featured clickers will hang in Seattle and multiply in cyberspace. Thanks to the mouse with the glowing ears we now have a chance to reinvent our bodies, just as it seemed that we might have to leave them behind in order to gain cyberspace. But our flesh can now compete with the virtual flesh. Our reality can stand up to virtuality, clicking its feelers, flapping its wings, baring its fangs, rippling its fur, and glowing. Just when it seemed that Borg was the way to go, the genetic playground opened up. Cyberspace, look out, the Geners are here!

Tech-Withdrawal Anxiety

You're in a foreign country, one of those little foreign countries just recently released from the damp basement of a dank and primitive past. Your hotel room with the soggy carpet and the tilting floor looks out onto an airshaft. Garbage flies regularly down and rats scurry at the bottom for indescribable scraps. The rotary phone doesn't work, and speaking into the lightbulb, which used to be the way to communicate in the damp old days, no longer pertains. The men who once sat patiently in a cement cubicle below your room listening breathlessly to your every breath have emigrated to a more technologically advanced country, yours let's say, in order to employ their gift for patient snooping in more rewarding ways. You are alone in your small room in this miserable damp small country at the far edge of nowhere, and there is no place to plug in your computer. There will be no phone calls, no e-mails, and certainly no snail mail for the duration of your stay, which, originally slated for one month, now looks more like an eternity.

After the first wave of tech-withdrawal anxiety has subsided, you ask yourself: And why should I, of all people, be so connected to other people that I must suffer withdrawal anxiety? The obvious answer is that you are neither important nor irreplaceable. If you disconnect from all the plugged-in people you used to be connected to, the network will make only an infinitesimal adjustment. No one will miss you. Your former plug-in mates will go on connecting with each other, barely noticing your absence. You realize then that the network is the most important thing. Anyone outside of it ceases to exist. You remember now, with some remorse, losing all your old epistolary friends for the simple reason that they wrote snail-mail letters, not e-mail. You dropped them into nonexistence, even though they were your oldest and best friends, because they were not plugged in. You pursued instead your newer, plugged-in acquintances, feeling as much at home as any chameleon. You are a technical parvenu.

When you realize this, you stick your head down the dark airshaft and, dodging rancid cabbage, shout down: "Anybody home?" and suddenly hundreds of heads appear in the shaft windows looking at you and jabbering in some nonelectronic language. The whole Third World is at home, which is quite reassuring and, while they start throwing spoiled foodstuffs at you, you are comforted by their physical proximity. Your plug doesn't love you enough to hit you with something smelly and squishy.